Living in 3D

Drink Drugs and Denial

Lorna Munro

Love to Maggie from Lorna xx

Published in 2020 by Ornum Press

ISBN Paperback: 978-1-8380671-0-6
Ebook: 978-1-8380671-1-3

A CIP catalogue copy of this book
can be found in the British Library.

Published with the help of Indie Authors World
www.indieauthorsworld.com

IndieAuthors
World

Dedication

I dedicate this book to my three daughters who are named in the book. I also dedicate it to my partner Robert who is my greatest support in life. Took eons to find him. I also dedicate it to families who have suffered and recovered who are still suffering from the effects of addictions to and from substances.

What readers thought

I read it twice!! First time in one sitting; I couldn't stop once I'd started. Second time, in three 'bytes' reflecting more on the 12 steps. I loved how each chapter reflected on the steps and Lorna's journey.

It is such an honest, authentic read. I was moved to tears. I identified strongly with so many of the themes discussed - the drinking culture in Scotland, the dramming, the sessions. The impact on the family when one or more person is alcohol dependent/ alcoholic, coming to terms openly with your feelings about everything, the denial, projection and dramas.

I really feel that Lorna has created a book which will be a support to anyone who is trying to come to terms with their relationship with alcohol.

At another level, it is the story of acceptance and learning to love yourself whole beyond judgements.

Jenny Anne Slater, Energy Alchemist & CEO of Forest Of The Stars Retreat, France.

An inspirational, authentic, deeply cathartic story and must read, for all those ensnared by Alcoholism, as well as the countless troubled family members in daily relationship with the Addicted individual

Mark Dempster, Addictions Counsellor, Author of *'Nothing to Declare: Confessions of an Unsuccessful Drug Smuggler, Dealer and Addict,* and *'The Ongoing Path: A Guide to Stopping Addictive Behaviour and Fulfilling Ambition'*

Acknowledgements

I would like to acknowledge some people who kept championing my journey with this book. In no particular order Nicole Mignone (https://www.facebook.com/NDMignone/) who read the book with some great feedback along with taking the photographs for the cover. She is an amazing writer herself and takes fantastic photographs while travelling, Pam MacLean who is great poet and writer, she also read the book giving feedback. I am delighted they took the time out to support me and read the book. Thank you so much ladies. I had family members who knew I was writing and kept encouraging me along the way. My aunt Joan is an inspiration as an author of five books herself. My other aunt Muriel kept encouraging me too. Other family members did not know I was writing yet I acknowledge them all as they were and continue to be great teachers in my life.

I have great friends Pauline Burnside (Artist) and Janet Norman who listened to my whines and wins and encouraged me always. I am in deep gratitude to a tribe I met on many courses in Lendrick Lodge where they too encouraged me to keep going. Too many names to mention here yet some are still in my life as long-time friends.

Thanks are due to Christine McPherson for her skills as an editor and to Kim and Sinclair Macleod of Indie Authors World who have made the publishing of this book possible.

My partner Robert is my biggest champion in life and has kicked me out of many comfort zones along the way with his encouragement and validation of what he sees as my genius. I would have given up long ago if not for him.

Introduction

Once upon a different life, I lived in a small homestead known as a village on a remote northerly coast in the Highlands of Scotland. This was what I would call a real community; a place where everyone would muck in together. One with a beach on either side of the village, rolling golden sands, and the Atlantic Ocean with all her differing moods ebbing and flowing to the dunes, and where we would jump down and race to her freezing breaths.

I was born in the swinging 60s, when a new spiritual revolution was exploding! In those days, we did not know anything about what living a spiritual life could mean. Even now, many of us may know about our physical selves, but what about our emotional and mental selves? Has anyone explained our spiritual selves to us?

Growing up, our teachers and the adults in our lives would tell us they knew what was right for us and what to do and what to think, using the principles and belief systems from their own education, parents, and culture. And the Highlands of Scotland were no exception.

It is said in many circles of self-help categories that we are spiritual beings having a human experience. First and foremost, here's the deal: we are here to have the human experience.

I believe that many of our experiences squash our spirit when we are children.

It is my intention to explain how my spirit fought its way to a point where, eventually, it gave up the battle with others, and the long and harrowing journey I took to reclaim it. I realised that I could share my own discoveries with others and maybe, hopefully, help someone somewhere, too!

It's a story which could be YOUR story. Or similar. And I would urge you to hear the similarities and not the differences. If you settle into your differences, you will resist hearing something that could help you.

By sharing the heights, depths, and widths of living in my shoes, I hope that some of you may identify with me in parts of my journey, and gain insight into ways to make your lives bearable until you can reach and heal the Spirit within you, to find the answers you seek, and the solutions to help you enjoy a happy life.

It is my wish that you may gain hope, courage, and strength through reading my story, and to know that you are not alone on your journey through life.

Watch how your body reacts as you read my story. Watch where you feel something in your body. Catch yourself when you feel you are judging and ask why that is.

Are you an addict? Yes? No? Remember, it is innate in humans to be addicted to something. This book is about my addictions, but you can change the words for your own. Maybe you don't realise you have any.

I have now learned that to really listen to others and hear them has been a major difficulty throughout my life. I was deaf to my own inner authority, so came to believe what others insisted were truths. As a child, I would feel something was not right but be told my feeling was wrong. So,

I interpreted this as meaning there was something wrong with me!

I'm no celebrity writing their autobiography. I am simply a human being sharing my journey, through situations and escapades where I have fallen many times... but somehow managed to get back up.

I am now blessed to have met someone who encourages me to write. Although he had very different circumstances growing up, this theme of alcoholism affected his life greatly, too.

I was raised around alcohol(ism) and brought the hell of it into my own immediate family, while he was brought up with the hell of it.

It is often suggested that by writing out our story, a catharsis may occur. And this is something I can identify with. I'm someone who notices that by taking a daily inventory of how I am in the world, the changes happen within me.

As this is a story of a dance with denial (the Devil, even), the real truth is that I'm scared, shit scared, of putting my story 'out there'. And this is my third attempt at writing this book. Deep down, I am still that frightened wee lassie who doesn't want to be told that what I'm feeling is stupid or not right, or that what I'm doing is crazy because others will criticise me. So, I used every distraction I could not to share my story.

But it was my partner who persuaded me that even if it would only help one person, my story and truth needed to be shared. For others to read, identify with, and understand. Then hopefully they will know that they too can come through any issues with or caused by alcohol, drugs, and the denial mask stuck in and around these substances, and to make a better life for themselves and their families and friends. I know many can't or don't want to, but just to have one person make changes can have a ripple effect on others.

My journey so far has not been an easy one. But it has certainly taught me a lot. And I can only desire that by finally sharing my experiences, thoughts, and feelings, I can in some way help others, too.

Let's start by explaining part of the title.

Drink ~ *take a liquid into the mouth and swallow. Alcohol ~ a colourless volatile flammable liquid which is the intoxicating constituent of wine, beer, spirits, and other drinks, and is also used as an industrial solvent and as fuel.*

First, I would like to say that I am neither in favour of nor against alcohol. It is a legal drug and I had many a good laugh and session with it. I do understand that there are many folks out there who continue to have a good time with alcohol, but I have seen and lived with the two sides of that coin.

It is a very seductive substance, and it took many years for me to understand this and to realise the destruction it has caused me personally and also within families, communities, and the world at large. It is said that if alcohol was to be taken out of society, 85% of mental disturbance would have a chance of recovery. I don't know if that is accurate, but I do agree that it would have a massive effect. Just take a walk around any city centre at the weekends and see the madness caused by consuming it.

I am sure we have all witnessed people change after consuming alcohol in ways that are unpleasant. We can laugh it off, yet it can be devastating for those who live with it.

Drug ~ *a medicine or other substance which has a physiological effect when ingested or otherwise introduced into the body.*

In many cases, we hear that drugs are used for medicinal purposes, and I believe there are many drugs out there that can help people. Me included.

The research I have carried out has been about my journey and what I have found to be true for me. Your story may be different.

I include alcohol as a drug. Although I dabbled with the other drugs – legal and illegal – my choice of drug was alcohol. The others only accompanied it at times.

Denial ~ *a statement that something is not true or does not exist.*

A statement that someone has not done something

~

'Denial is the shock absorber for the Soul. It protects us until we are equipped to cope with reality.' C.S. Lewis

American self-help author Melody Beattie calls denial 'the fertile breeding ground for the behaviours we call co-dependent, controlling, focusing on others, and NEGLECTING ourselves' and believes that 'illness and compulsive or addictive behaviours can also emerge during denial'.

However, in her view, 'the first step towards acceptance is denial. The first step towards moving THROUGH denial is accepting that we may be in denial, and then GENTLY allowing ourselves to move through.'

Humans go through specific phases from birth to teenage years, and at certain times some of us may have turned to drink and/or drugs. Some outgrew these tendencies while others continued with them until their lives became unmanageable.

I always insisted, 'I enjoy my smoke, I enjoy a drink, I enjoy a cigarette.' Yet really, when I look back, I realise that for the majority of the time I didn't. It was just easier to say that to someone who was dictating to me about the health risks, etc, and to get them off my back. Basically, I was saying, 'Fuck off and mind your own business.'

Of course, I would say that, too! It came back to being told what I should or should not be doing. Instant rebellion!

There is every likelihood that you will know someone who has an issue with alcohol or drugs. Maybe you have an issue yourself.

But there are many different types of abuse nowadays which could be offshoots from these two. And denial lives within them all! Take technology, for instance. It is ramping up so quickly that our children are becoming addicted to phones and to gaming. And not, it would seem, just children. I admit I have my mobile phone with me all the time, using the excuse of needing it for work. However, I am aware of this, and try to be diligent in rationing myself over how much time I use it to check out social media. Balance again.

When I first started to write this book, I tended to be very negative about my past. I was still mentally distorted in my thinking that my story would easily have come across as all doom and gloom – and it certainly has been anything but that! But after a workshop on creative writing, I deleted everything and started again. And as I delved into my memory banks, I started to see both sides of my story – the positive and negative; the yin and the yang.

Unfortunately, some families have endured awful experiences that I could not even begin to imagine coping with. Yet I have come to realise that two people could be watching the same movie and have totally different perspectives on it. This is just part of life. As we all have unique fingerprints, we are also unique as individuals. So, where one family member sees a truth, the other would deny it.

I had no idea I was living in denial for years, and when I finally had the awakening from that place, I hit a depression. A grieving process was needed about the person I thought I was, because I believed I was someone that my parents, other family members, schoolteachers, religious leaders, and others had always told me I was. How rude for anyone else to preach to us about who we are, eh? Surely it would be much better for others to guide us to find out who we are.

Then again, how could we be guided, when the people who walked before us had been told who they were? Scott Peck, who wrote The Road Less Travelled, says that 'dysfunctional parents will create dysfunctional children'. And so it goes on.

I do not want to lay blame on anyone, as I have grown to know that I have created my life with the tools I was given at any particular time, and I use the tools I continue to find. Many others have come into my life these past 18 years who have shown me that I am 100% accountable and responsible for MY life – and only MY life.

At the times I birthed my daughters into the world, I had no idea I had been programmed to think in particular ways. As we grow throughout our adult lives, we change our minds about things and say, 'If I only knew then what I know now.'

In each phase of a child's life, we need different tools and skills. Yet to love unconditionally is the best we can do. Many of us do not understand that concept or have not experienced it for ourselves, so how can we offer it to our children? We experience cuddles from caregivers when we do as they want, yet they are not forthcoming when we misbehave.

From their earliest years, our children watch and learn, listen and learn. Our job is to show them how to look after their bodies, show them socially acceptable skills, and let them know we are their caretakers... at least until later, when hopefully we have guided them to take care of themselves and we let them go.

Also, in the early years of a child's life, they need to be given lots of nourishment with cuddles and hugs, teaching and guidance, understanding and patience. But as they grow, they require their parents to offer emotional space, to listen with an open heart (hEARt), with respect, and to trust them to live independently by letting go without judging their choices.

A wise woman told me that the teachers of the future are teachers of experience, and these are the people I now hang out with. Like-minded souls, who do not judge my crazy thinking, who may or may not have had similar experiences, but we are willing to trust each other.

No-one truly knows what goes on behind the eyes of another, even if their experience is similar. Yet we can have an understanding, share a hug, and offer a listening and sympathetic ear to another. That is kindness – and we ALL love a bit of that, don't we?

'Those who cling to views and perceptions, wander the world offending each other.'
Buddha

Chapter One
November 2001

'Who am I supposed to be again? Just be yourself.
But who am I?'

Candace Bushnell

Who am I? Do I even know the answer to this question? I asked myself this on a daily basis at that time, and also wrote it down in my journal. I was 38 years of age, nearing 39.

This was not the first time I had thought of killing myself, but this time it felt more likely. I wrote in my diary the best way to do this. I believed if I bought a 40oz bottle of vodka and a few packets of paracetamol, that should do it. But when would I do it? And how could I be sure no-one would find me? Because the thought of being found and brought back, and then living like a vegetable... on and on these thoughts raced, until finally I would fall asleep. Albeit a very restless sleep.

This was my nightly ritual of believing that suicide would be the best way out for me and, of course, for my kids. They were resilient, I reckoned, so they would get over it! For f#ck's sake, they would be better off; their dad lived round the corner, so they would be ok! At one stage, when I was married to their dad, I had pondered the suicide route and told myself I would have to take the children with me. Was I madder then or now? I did not even believe this was crazy thinking. I was really starting to believe this would be the best option for everyone concerned. Oh, poor, poor me!

My demise did not happen physically at first, although it was physical pain that triggered my internal and spiritual 'death'. I suspect it was already there, covered by masks of denial which would need to be peeled off later one by one. At that time, I was functioning, appeared ok, and played a wonderful part of being self-assured and confident to the outside world... or so I believed. Everyone is so wrapped up with their own 'stuff', maybe they saw through that or maybe they didn't.

Some of my friends had disappeared, and I would lose myself in my work by day and telly and soap operas by night, puffing on cannabis joints or cigarettes to numb my fast-paced thoughts!

I was certainly addicted to adrenalin. The drama drug! I believe that humans are pre-programmed for addiction, and our minds are the best place for this to start. The addiction creeps in and you don't even notice, so it is easy to deny it when someone questions you. Adrenalin addiction is one of the subtler addictions that many of us may not even know we have. That familiarity becomes the norm; unacceptable behaviour becomes the acceptable!

I was prescribed anti-depressants, but returned to the GP after four weeks, complaining they did not work. I was then given another prescription, and it was hinted that I may need psychiatric help! What? Me need to speak with a psychiatrist? Now, that was funny. I knew all about those types of doctors and I didn't need to see one.

If my partner at that time would just stop drinking, everything would be ok, I told myself. I just needed 'something' to help my head to slow down. On occasions, I would be prescribed Valium, which did do the trick. My thoughts would seem to slow down and I appeared to make better decisions for a short while.

I would only ever want two weeks' supply and try to make them last longer, unless my partner at that time found them and he would take them. I always felt embarrassed about going to the doctor and asking for medication, as I had been through so many different kinds. The last one I was ever prescribed was Prozac!

Counselling was another avenue I went down, although by that stage I felt I had pretty much exhausted it in the previous five years. I wanted someone to fix me, yet at the same time I bitterly complained there was nothing wrong with me so why did I need to go to counselling in the first place?

On one occasion I went to see a psychotherapist who helps to uncover your past, yet I was in no mental state at that time to continue. In the end, I found any excuse not to go on with it – not enough money, or no sitters to watch the kids when they were on holiday from school.

I also went with my then partner to see a relationship counsellor, but he arrived drunk so she wouldn't see us. And the following week, she actually challenged me! Or at least that's the way it felt to me from the questions she was asking, and the smirk I reckoned I detected on my partner's face. I wanted him sorted out, not me. So, that was it for me; I decided we were not going back there.

Then there was the counsellor I saw at the Alcohol Counselling place. It was near my home, so I always felt highly embarrassed sneaking in, and especially out, in case anyone would see me. My mind was on constant hyper-alert, believing people were looking at me. It was classic victimhood, although I did not know anything about that back then. And when you throw in some paranoia and neurosis, it makes a real live cocktail of mental disturbance!

Some people noticed a change in me, because I recall a friend saying to me, 'It's good to have you back' when we were on a night out after I had been in recovery for some time. I replied that I had been back (from living abroad) for some years, but she said, 'No, it's good to have YOU back.' Of course, what she meant was the freedom-seeking Lorna who liked to party and drink. Even then, my behaviour was not the real me. It was a learned behaviour, which I would have to realise later on. A behaviour led through the spirit of alcohol – the wrong kind of spirit.

I only liked attending the Alcohol Counselling because it gave me the opportunity to unload all my grievances about my partner, as close friends and family were fed up hearing my moans. They kept telling me that if I was so unhappy, I should end the relationship. I could not seem to do that, although I had the deep intuition that they were right. They were giving me well-meaning advice, as friends do, yet I could not end it. I was riddled with fear; it was oozing out of me like a Swiss cheese!

It didn't help that I wasn't able to tell my family the truth about how I felt inside, mainly because I didn't really know how I felt myself. I convinced myself that if this man I was living with would stop drinking, the drama and violence would then stop, and we could all get on with being a family unit – a happy family. When he was not on an alcohol binge, it appeared as though we were all ok. But we weren't really.

It was my mission to make happiness happen, and I tried every way I knew. It was my obsession; my childish dream of a happy-ever-after fairy tale. How could I know then that I was still this little girl inside an adult body? An adult-child.

So, there had to be a few more dramas before I became sick and tired of being sick and tired. One day, as I was leaving a friend's house sporting a black eye and wearing a baseball cap with my head hanging down, I ran into someone who gave me hope! He suggested I try the sister fellowship of Alcoholics Anonymous. I immediately said that I wasn't an alcoholic, but he replied, 'No, this is for the friends and relatives of alcoholics.' Luckily, that was the seed planted for me.

Another month or two passed and another drama ensued before I would contact anyone.

Chapter Two
April 2002

'The secret of getting ahead is getting started.'
Agatha Christie

I picked up the phone book and dialled the number that had been suggested to me. I don't really remember what I said, but a very nice woman took my number and said she would have someone call me back.

The 'someone' called, and as I spilled out my sorry story, she seemed to totally understand me. I couldn't believe that here was another person who had experienced similar goings-on in her life and was holding her hand out to offer me help! I always thought that if I promised to do something then I had to carry that out. I felt this was one of those times when I had to do just that and agree to anything. At that point, I was not looking for any differences; that would come later. It was all suggested to me without any 'shoulds or shouldn'ts' thrown into the conversation. How cool was that! I was simply told how it worked and that it was up to me to make a decision or not whether to go. For once, it was an invitation not an instruction.

No-one had ever done this before. No-one had shared their experiences with me and explained how a support group had worked for them. I needed someone to hear me and acknowledge me, to recognise who I was and support me while I unravelled, not to tell me what to do. Even with good intentions, I was not and never had been very good at taking what I perceived to be orders. And I constantly needed approval to be validated from another human being.

One of my biggest problems was that I could not just end a relationship or leave a situation. I would always try to fix it or hang onto it, to show I could fix it or make it better. I would become emotionally attached to some people and try to change our relationship – even becoming co-dependent.

In all honesty, I was useless at emotions and had no clue how to work with them maturely. I tended to find another emotional cripple, and we would try and hold each other up.

A few days later, I was outside a community building waiting for someone to meet me. When they did not appear, I was desperate enough to pluck up the courage to ring the bell, and a very nice lady came and welcomed me in.

There were 17 people there that night (I counted them) and I was screaming on the inside that I wanted to leave, but some stories were keeping me rigid in my seat. I was squashing down the rising tears; I couldn't let people see me cry.

I heard God being mentioned, and freaked out on the inside! God? Oh God! What have I come into here? They're all 'Holy Willies'! They're talking about God and I cannot be here with that kind of talk! Wait a minute, I thought. I had promised the woman on the phone I would come to six of these meetings before I would make my mind up if they were for me or not, yet I had decided there and then that they were most definitely NOT! Then came the inner beating-up I was so good at: Why did I agree to come here for six meetings? Why can't I learn to shut up instead of agreeing to do something right away? Why am I so damn stupid?

At the end, a lady came to me and asked if I had heard anything I could relate to, and then the floodgates opened. I cried, 'Oh my God! He's an alcoholic!' But I couldn't separate myself from my then partner. He was my obsession. An addiction even.

She comforted me and invited me to come back the following week, and I agreed. This woman was probably around the same age as my mum, so I felt I had to respect my elders and keep my word.

The following week, I returned – very reluctantly, I have to say.

I was invited to speak, but I could only say my name, and hated every minute of the beginning of this support group meeting. I had no idea why I was there, except that I could relate to things some of the people were saying. Unfortunately, I kept focusing on the fact that they mentioned God, which was just the start of me looking for differences.

Then, the second time around, I heard someone say, 'When I first came here, I hated the fact that God was mentioned.' Wait a minute, what did that lady just say? I thought. Oh! That's exactly how I think! That was a turning point for me, although I did not realise it just yet.

So, I started to listen to what this lady had to say. At last someone was making complete sense to me. But why did she stay when she felt like I did? This piqued my curiosity, yet I was too scared to ask. (This was really resistance to someone who could help.) As I listened to her, I really resonated with how she felt about things while she had lived with an alcoholic. She was not with that man any more, which intrigued me. But she was now with someone else who was a self-confessed alcoholic, who she had not known in drink.

I so wanted this to be me, yet I wanted it to be me and my then partner so that we could be the perfect fairytale-ending couple.

There were slogans and motivational sayings dotted around the room, but they didn't impress me. God was mentioned there, too, and I saw one which my mother would often say to me as a teenager: 'This too shall pass!' God, how I loathed that saying! Now it's one I love and use a lot, even the good events in life will pass...

In the end, I did go for the six weekly meet-ups, and one night at home I felt myself thinking of one of these slogans. There was an argument going on in the sitting room while I was in the kitchen, and I could hear my name being screamed by both my partner and my children. Think, think, think (one of the slogans), Lorna. And it gave me breathing space to respond.

I was overcome with sensations in my body I could not control on the inside – a lurching stomach, tingling I did not recognise, my heart thudding in my chest. What was this? That was the first time I had asked my body that question. I had been aware of the knot in my gut on many occasions and had felt my heart racing in some circumstances, yet I had never really FELT it before. And I certainly had never asked what it was.

The argument in the sitting room, which I suspect is a common occurrence within family homes, was about who was watching what on the TV. Normal family stuff, yes? Not in our home, though, because it could lead to someone storming out and getting drunk. It could end up with screaming and shouting, and things being thrown, or holes being made in walls or doors. Then all hell would break loose! The police might come! Children could be so scared they'd hide in cupboards with the family cat!

This time, though, I quietly asked them all what was happening, and was met with a barrage of words from three kids and an adult (or was it four kids?). 'Mam, tell him to...' and 'Tell your kids to...' But for once, I responded rather than reacted. I replied that I was busy in the kitchen and would appreciate if they could sort it out amongst themselves. Sounds perfectly easy, doesn't it? Yes, even writing this now, it does. So, why was it not easy?

My heart was pounding so hard I believed they would hear it, or that it would jump out of my chest. But when I returned to the kitchen a shaking wreck, I noticed that everything had gone quiet in the sitting room. What the hell? Confused, I thought of an excuse to go back into the room, and to my surprise I found them all watching something together – and laughing! I asked if anyone wanted a drink of juice or tea, and they all answered 'no thanks' and carried on as if there had been no argument.

Peace prevailed in the home! Stunned, I asked myself: What just happened there? I could clearly imagine what would have happened in the past if I had not had this small slogan to refer to! I would have reacted very differently, and the scenario would have turned out to be much different.

But this showed me MY behaviour, and I was starting to view ME, not anyone else. These meetings I was attending were instilling the idea of 'Let it begin with me'.

Previously, I would have thrown down the dishes, stormed into the room, and screamed at the kids to go to their rooms because they had their own TV, and my then partner would have got his way. The kids would have hated me, and he would have been smiling. OR, he would have stormed out to the pub, leaving me in a foul mood, which I would have taken out on the kids and blamed them for making him leave.

Wow! What a revelation! And there were many more of them to come.

Was I starting to feel better? I believed so. These meetings had become my weekly sanctuary where I could relax and know I was in a safe environment. I found myself becoming excited the day before I was due to attend a meeting, and I felt our home was quieter, the girls more upbeat, and the arguments had calmed down. What you would call a typical family home. Of course, this would be short-lived, yet it was so much better than before. And if I happened to miss a meeting, I felt it – and so did everyone around me!

I had been given phone numbers to call, and I started to open up a bit more about my life. A lovely woman came over at the end of one of the meetings and shared her story with me. I warmed to her immediately and was so intrigued that I asked if we could meet for a coffee.

I was great at talking on a one-to-one basis, but still found it hard to open up completely as I realised I wouldn't or couldn't trust anyone too much. I was even starting to realise that this God they talked about could be whatever I wanted It to be! I liked that idea, but realised I felt guilty about it. Why was I feeling guilty? I was starting to name my feelings. Or was I naming my thoughts about my feelings? Some days I would think it was all just too difficult, yet it was certainly better than the way I had been living previously.

I was a 200-mile per hour person in distraction from the truth of who I really was. I loved to be out at work so that I did not have to spend time in my home, albeit things were improving there.

Then my partner stopped drinking!

Chapter Three
December 2002

'A child is an uncut diamond.'
Austin O'Malley

I kept going back to these meetings and started to understand more about what was happening. It helped me to become stronger, and I found the courage to buy my flat and a better car. My partner had only managed to stop drinking for three months, but at least there was hope. And hope was proving to be my new medication at that time.

I was encouraged to keep coming to the meetings and to share my experience, my strength, and my hope. Eventually, that hope helped me to come off all anti-depressants, as it was proving to be far better than any of the tablets I had thrown down my neck.

I kept up my journalling, which was vital for me, as I realised reading back over the year how utterly obsessed I was with what others were doing, especially my partner. Strangely, there was no mention in my journals of what I was doing, other than bitching and blaming and complaining how bad the world and everyone in it was TO me!

The outside smiley face was a mask I could put on, and I would change my masks to suit the occasion or situation I found myself in. A true chameleon. A small mouse inside me, a lion roaring on the outside. If you ever watched the TV series Wurzel Gummidge, he had a few heads in his cupboard and would choose one to put on to suit the occasion. So, I was like him in that respect.

I was feeling stronger, though, and found the courage to separate physically from my partner, although the relationship was kept going on my terms. I didn't realise that I was still trying to be in control of the relationship, yet this was a new level. I was starting a journey within myself, looking at me while still looking outwards and wanting the change to be there. I had no idea the change needed to be within me.

I continued with the weekly meetings and daily readings, and would phone two particular ladies from the group when I found myself in a place of sadness, anger, or fear. I did do this often, to be honest. Surprisingly, I had managed to get over my inner chatter of 'Oh, don't bother them' and 'What if they can't be arsed talking with you?' or 'You're just a burden to people, can't you see that?' That was my inner dialogue in the beginning, but someone at some point in one of the meetings would comment on exactly what I had been thinking, and that intrigued me so much that I kept coming back.

The relationship was on and it was off; my partner was in and he was out. And I realised I still could not make boundaries for myself or my children.

I began attending conventions and soaking up whatever knowledge I could from people. Although I was in Al-Anon – the group for friends and families of alcoholics – I decided to also go along to open Alcoholics Anonymous meetings to learn about the disease.

What many people do not realise is that these two fellowships are very different in their approaches. AA is for the alcoholic themselves; Al Anon is for the friends and relatives of the alcoholic. The only requirement for membership in AA is that there be a problem with alcohol; the only requirement for membership in Al Anon is that there be a problem with alcohol for a friend or relative (where this is causing YOU distress). In some parts of the USA, it is – or was – compulsory to attend these meetings if going into a caring career like nursing, or anywhere where addictions were attached to their choice of work. It is not so in the UK.

I read many stories about people who would attend a meeting with their friend as a support, then hear something they identified with themselves and continue going along even when their friend stopped. And the meetings are attended by all sorts of different people. Everyone is treated as equals, and I liked that! Even the minority had a voice.

Alcoholism and addiction are worldwide issues, and I honestly believe that mental illness would improve if alcohol was taken out of society, after witnessing its effects.

November 2007

Five years later, and I was still attending meetings, even though I had initially said I was only going to go along to the six. By that time, I had a good grasp of the 12 Step Programme. The first one was started by Bill Wilson as AA, then adapted by his wife and friends 15 years later. I loved it.

My girls would comment if I missed any meetings, as my old patterns of behaviour would resurface when I was not consistent with following this new way of looking at life. It was still taking time for the fog to lift from my mind, to change my behaviour and attitude, and I was still seeing my then partner even though we did not live together. Hindsight tells me this kept me from speedy recovery, along with needing to peel off layers of the denial mask.

I was becoming frustrated, so went back to the GP and asked for Valium, only to be told this was a common occurrence at this time of year. I dug out my journals again and sifted through them, and realised she was right!

The problem seemed to be that my partner's drinking had gone up a notch around October, changing my state of mind and thinking, which made me run around to distract myself yet again. Denial was deep!

But I really wanted to do these steps! I'd understood them on an intellectual level, but what would it mean to study them deeply at another level? I was sick and tired again!

I'd bought my flat, got a better car – still a banger – and changed my job, but I was still miserable on the inside! I could not seem to make decisions to help myself get out of this destructive relationship. Why could I not end it once and for all? I knew it was affecting my life, and not for the better. Some days, we would be ok, but I wanted more than ok. I wanted to feel happy! In all honesty, I hardly saw him anyway, because I'd told him that he could not be around me while he was on a drinking binge, and that was more often than not. The relationship was more mental/ emotional than physical.

I found the saying 'one day at a time' damn near impossible to incorporate into my life, because I was always projecting forward or looking back and would never know when enough was enough. Although I had managed to put the daily practice into my work, I still hadn't done so in other areas of my life yet.

Even when I had a run of better days, I was still not satisfied, yet I knew these steps offered a solution. One of the sayings in the fellowship was 'You're as sick as your secrets', but I had no idea what that meant.

I was about to find out!

That particular month, I was quiet at my weekly meetings. I felt stuck again. I was noticing that the month of November always seemed to be a contemplating sort of month for me. And my life was so complex.

I told myself that my then partner would not survive without me, yet he was actually doing that just fine! I also realised that I knew deep within me I did not want to have a relationship with him any more. I did not want to fix him, or our lives to be this illusionary happy family. So, why then could I not just say, 'I do not want to see or be with you any more'? It sounds so simple now on writing this, but back then I could not muster up the emotional maturity to utter the words. It would mean having to really FEEL.

I knew my heart was telling me to do just that, but this head of mine kept finding some other reason not to! I was convinced that the pain inside would kill me if I succumbed to it. I had no idea I was incapable of feeling my feelings. I had named them, yes, but to feel them was another matter!

I was experiencing 'living grief' for an illusionary relationship with someone alive. Yet really, he was not living either. He was existing in a hell of his own making, too. A living grief for the Lorna I believed I was, which was more important.

TRUTH: I was avoiding myself! I was avoiding looking deeper into my heart. Deeper into places I knew I was not going to like. I was trying to cling onto who I believed I was rather than letting her go completely.

Then one night after a meeting, I was pacing the floor at home. I had text out a shitty message to my partner and had my thumb hovering over the 'send' button. Inside my mind, there was a raging war going on, knowing that my action was not appropriate. Then I heard a voice inside shouting, 'PHONE ROSEMARY!' I Ignored it!

When I had been about to do similar things before, I'd phone someone from the fellowship and chat with them about how I was feeling – or what I was thinking! And it had always proved a reliable way to deal with making sure no-one would be upset or misinterpret anything.

However, that night I was about to press 'send' when I heard the voice again, 'PHONE ROSEMARY'.

She was a lady from the Central belt of Scotland whom I had met at conventions. And although I knew she would be good for me, I had so far avoided phoning her, even though she had suggested I did. She had issued the invitation to me many times, yet I had always resisted. It was always these moments or actions I avoided that always turned out to be good for my progress when I finally acted upon them. Gosh, I was such a slow learner!

So, I phoned Rosemary! And in the 90 minutes that we chatted, I learned more about how this 12 Step Programme worked than in all the six years of attending meetings.

She asked me where I was in my recovery and with the programme, but I had no idea what she meant. She decided we would just chat and see where it took us.

The meetings I had been attending were my lifeline at that time, yet I always wanted more. I always felt there was more. But it was all to do with me! Was I listening? Yes! Was I hearing? Not always. There's a big difference!

TRUTH: My mind had become so screwed up that I needed that six years of regular meetings for my mind to slowly change and have the beginnings of a spiritual emergence.

The ladies who were helping me at my home group could see what I couldn't, and it triggered my impatience. Deep down, I just knew things, yet my head would catch me out at every turn. It was the driver of my life and took over every situation. Yet I knew my heart knew what was good for me and that I should take the driving seat!

It was explained that it was a spiritual programme, not a religious one, and to find a Higher Power that suited me. So, I slowly sacked the God of my understanding and I hired a new one. One whom I could relate to. One that was not going to punish me if I was a 'bad girl'. I did not realise, though, that I was about to embark on tackling where all these thoughts had come from.

I asked Rosemary if she would be my sponsor, and her reply was, 'I'd be delighted to help you in any way I can.'

I was delighted, yet she had not actually agreed to be my sponsor! I wanted an aye or a no, but she had not given me that. I didn't realise I still could not make a healthy decision for myself!

TRUTH: I did not understand that my ego-mind was strong and determined to have its own way! I did not understand that I always had to be right! I did not understand that I was full of fear! I did not understand very much!

Rosemary asked me if I had a particular book from the Al Anon literature, and if not, to get it and answer the questions on the first chapter, then email her my answers by December.

'Oh no,' I replied, 'I intend to do a step a month next year. So, if you don't mind, I'll do it in January!'

She gave a wee laugh and said, 'You asked me to help, so if you can just do that, please.'

In that moment, I agreed. But inside, I was thinking, Wait a minute, did she just tell me to do something? I'll do it in January.

Still Lorna's will.

~

Back to my Roots - February 1963

We lived in a small community where there were probably more sheep than people! Situated in the scenic county of Sutherland on the north coast of the Scottish Highlands, with golden beaches and majestic mountains.

This was in the 'swinging 60s' which were named as the most defining decade of the 20th century, when post-war 'baby boomers' (young men & women growing up immediately after the Second World War) came of age. The generation we entered into was Generation X, although these generations overlap. Some say WE were the baby boomers!

The Beatles sang 'All You Need Is Love', and flower power was rife. It was the years of the sexual revolution and peace-seekers like Martin Luther King and John F Kennedy fell to the assassins' bullets. Neil Armstrong landed on the moon. Marilyn Monroe, the American actress, singer and model, became a sex siren with a troubled past, and was found dead with a 'possible suicide' sensationalised. The contraceptive pill came to fruition in the 60s, and I believe this may just be the era when 'celebrity-ism' (maybe not a dictionary word, but one I use) came into play and people became obsessed with singers like Elvis Presley, the Beatles, and the Rolling Stones, to name a few, and they became little gods whom the public idolised!

Now I realise I played everything down that occurred in my life, due to a few factors. I had a good childhood in the physical sense. I was well nurtured as the daughter of parents who, I suspect (and this would be denied), would have preferred a boy. You know, that bullshit about the 'heir to the throne' or 'carrying the family name on' and how it could only be done through having a son. First son inherits all! I went on to have three daughters, and always felt pretty useless because I could not produce a son, although my mother told me the only one who was disappointed when I had my last daughter was my father. Now I know this thinking to be ludicrous. I'd also like to point out that my dad loved all my daughters, as did my mother. However, this comment actually made me feel even less worthy. Mam did not know this, of course. Neither of us had the awareness to know that these belief systems (BS) were bull shit! (BS)

Don't get me wrong. I am certain that the family was really delighted that I was a healthy girl, because my poor mam had to endure a hard labour with me as a breech birth back then. No C-sections to make an easier landing pad! She had been taken into hospital in Inverness – a long way from the wee village where she lived – and was stuck there with complete bed rest for four months until I arrived in February 1963, the day after a full moon, and sucking my thumb. Mam told me that nurses from other wards came to see the baby that had been born with her thumb in her mouth.

Psychologists have something to say about why babies and children do this. It's said it is a comforter for the baby, which then becomes a habit. That seems to me a logical reason. In chirology (hand reading) it is said that the thumb represents the flow of 'chi' which comes from God (Source, Higher Power, whatever name you give It), and the concept of the sucking motion says we are drinking nourishment from Spirit. So, it comforts the child. Both of these reasons make sense to me, and I sucked my thumb until I was a teenager. Then I continued with a new habit. Smoking.

My experimentation with the spirit of alcohol started as a teenager. According to Freud, this would relate to issues with aggression and dependency. This was another Truth for me, as I ended up studying various psychologies and becoming eclectic with my knowing of which was true for me. Please research for your own self what is true for you. Remember the similarities, though! Only if you feel you need to.

I hated smoking, yet my best friend did it, others were doing it, and I wanted to fit in. We started in the shed with my best friend's mother's full-strength Capstans, which had no filter on the tip. I did not like confrontation and did not manage to shout louder at that stage of my life, because I wanted approval from those I loved. So, I learned to people-please. I found out later that my best friend was my first soul mate; my first 'love', so to speak. I adored her and she me, and we did everything together. She lived next door to my gran, and all my time was spent with her whenever possible.

I can look back now and see that I adhered to whatever she wanted me to do, because she would not speak to me if I didn't. In the usual way that children fall out, we would glare at each other, throw our heads back, roll our eyes to the heavens, and scowl. Eventually, I would get fed up and try everything in my power to please her and convince her to speak to me again. Sometimes, to no avail.

I now feel this set me up to pick men in my life who would sulk in the same way, which meant communication was difficult.

I'm not blaming anyone here, just pointing to directions that set me up for adulthood with the choices I made. No-one made me make these choices but myself. Kids fall out all the time.

This hurt my sensitivity so much that I would suppress my feelings again and do things I did not really want to do. In adults, this could be viewed as passive- aggressive behaviour, along with some bullying tactics, but as children we have no idea about these behaviours. I am eternally grateful to all the people who came into my life on this earth at this time, for the gifts I have had from them. You see, I eventually learned that no-one does anything TO us; it is all FOR us, but ONLY IF we embark on the journey of our Soul. This is what it means to look inside of ourselves.

I was the first grandchild on Mam's side of the family, and the youngest on Dad's side at that time. So, I was adored on both sides. I did tend to spend more time with family on Mam's side, though. On occasions, we would visit my dad's uncle, who would have a £1 note and a bar of Dairy Milk in the drawer for me every time. I thought I was rich! He always wore dark clothes and a bunnet (hat) on his head as he sat puffing on a pipe in the dark. There was always smoke belching from the chimney back into the room. That is my memory of him and our visits.

He was the last of Dad's uncles, and I don't recall hearing anything about this side of the family other than Dad telling me he used to have to go and get an uncle from the pub; he was called 'Hard Rock', and had an alcohol issue. Dad also told me that as a wee laddie he would sit on the stairs watching his dad and friends 'dramming' (drinking alcohol), and that his mother hated drink and had turned to the Bible.

In society we have many labels – I could have a number of them when I study the 'symptoms' laid out for certain behaviours. I have the label of being an HSP – a highly sensitive person. As a child, I knew a lot but was told I was wrong or to stop thinking so daft. I suppose that's okay, because that's what adults say to children. In my view, children are treated as a collective more than individuals. They are herded into schools, dressed like minions, and told what to think, instead of being encouraged to play or asked what they think or, more importantly, feel. Perhaps some of you feel they didn't have that experience, but I did. Even though I had some lovely teachers, I always felt I fell foul of the ones who, in my opinion, either disliked children or hated their profession and were in the wrong job!

I recall my first day in school. I was four-and-a-half years old and running up the corridor, when a large (to me) man with a cane under his arm roared at me that he would belt me if he caught me running up the corridor again. Boom! Was that the day I stopped running for fun? Maybe.

I ran home to Mam, sobbing that I didn't want to go back to that place. She went and fought on my behalf, and so the stage was set. Mam was always fighting my corner, and I became co-dependent. At the age of four, it's a good thing for a Mam or Dad to fight their kid's corner. But unfortunately, I took this into adulthood. For many years, poor Mam took all my problems and would try to fix them for me. I think she would do anything for a quiet life.

I was very tall for my age, so I believe that expectations were put upon me. But as a highly sensitive child, I would cry and get angry at the boys who would pull my hair (as boys did back then, and possibly still do) and call me names. Then I would be told, 'Sticks and stones will break your bones, but names will never harm you.'

What rubbish! Clearly, I felt harmed by their name-calling or else I would not have been crying. I would implode until I had to explode. I would suppress the cries because 'big girls don't need to cry'. All these feelings were held inside, festering as resentments to be unleashed in adulthood.

When I was around 11 years old, two major events happened. One was that I started menstruating, and the other was my beloved grandfather died. I was excited about the former and devastated by the latter.

I have no memory of how my mother fed me information about my period, yet I do recall whispers amongst the adults when Papa died. We arrived by train to be picked up by my aunt. When we rounded the corner to my aunt's home, and I saw the undertaker's car parked outside, I immediately started screaming, because I knew my papa was dead. Hysterical, I was taken to my gran, who slapped me... then comforted me on her knee, as she always did. She explained that Papa was now with the angels in heaven, and told me why she'd had to slap me.

So, once again, my true feelings were slapped down and repressed. Perhaps my gran could not handle her own emotions and those of her daughters and sons, and the way she dealt with them was to supress them, perhaps crying in bed alone. I don't know, yet I see that is what I grew up doing a lot. I was extremely highly emotional, though, and would whoop and wail a lot.

However, the change in perception with that story is that my mother says it is not true. She says that I knew before we got on the train that my papa was dead. Yet I still believe it happened the way I remember. So, we will have to agree to disagree here.

I have looked again and again at my past. I believe that I was a reactive repressive type who experienced raw emotions, and I made decisions according to these emotions, which is what shaped my life. I also believe that my mother was an HSP and found it difficult to cope with a highly sensitive, emotionally-impaired child/ adolescent! Maybe not all the time, but certainly a lot of the time.

Because I could not handle confrontation, I shouted louder than the people who raised their voices. I had a mixture of a reactive and repressive nature. My father was quite authoritarian in his approach, probably because he had experienced that himself as the youngest of five, and with three big sisters. My mam was certainly authoritative in her approach, as the eldest of three sisters and with two younger brothers. And she would threaten me with my dad. I'm sure a lot of us were brought up with the threat of 'wait till your father gets home!' It's the way it was back then, but it did instil repression.

I actually received my first 'thrashing' – as it was called then – by my mam when I was only three years old. I had disappeared with my friend to the hills, and the whole village had been out looking for us. We were eventually found on top of a hill, which to the adults seemed extremely dangerous for little children.

My memory of that day was of sunshine and joy... until I saw my mam in a car with others shouting my name, and I just knew in that moment I was in trouble. As children, we use what is known as the sixth sense, so I just knew. And I was so afraid that I left my shoes and socks up on the hill.

Mam explained to me afterwards why she had done it, but I now know this instilled in me a fear of embarrassment and humiliation, due to the thrashing happening in public. Nowadays, of course, a 'thrashing' would be deemed as physical abuse towards a child.

But at that stage of my life, I was being taught that physical and emotional pain was for my own good. Unfortunately, this held me in that repressive place and allowed it to manifest through violence later in life. I always felt that punishments dished out by adults were 'for my own good' and that everything they told me must be right. Even when it did not FEEL right to me.

Within the confines of my support group I learned that I needed to study the steps because they were essential for progress. I learned I was a work in progress, so I was ready to really knuckle down and study them.

I now invite you to walk through the steps with me.

Chapter Four
January 2008

'The pain of powerlessness is excruciating. It is the most painful experience in the earth school, and everyone shares it.'

Gary Zukav

STEP 1: 'We admitted we were powerless over alcohol and our lives had become unmanageable.'

I had asked a lovely lady to be my sponsor when I first entered the rooms of the Al Anon Family Groups. The truth is that she reminded me of my mam; she would say I reminded her of her daughter. Even though I resisted a lot of what she would say to me, deep down I knew it to be true. Even when she would straight-line things with me in the most loving way she could, I would still fight her every step of the way. I did not realise that she, too, was a soul mate, someone who would challenge me, who would stir up those shadows within me. I had a love-hate relationship with her, yet she kept on loving me. I say hate, but it was only my own resistance to her help. I would also go from her to another lady who, I felt, was much gentler in her approach AND would always back me up with my opinions. She didn't really challenge me.

I took my first step! I got and devoured every piece of literature I could find on the subject, then posted my answers to Rosemary. I then realised that I had admitted it, yet I had not truly accepted it. Gee-whiz! I had taken 5-6 years now for that step to find its way into my psyche.

I was powerless over what others did, how they thought, how they behaved. Boom! Another revelation! I had not even noticed my life was unmanageable. Until then, I had believed I was managing it just grand, thank you very much, and that I was managing others' lives, too, if only they would let me. My God! How had I missed that? I had managed to accept I was powerless over my partner's drinking yet not that MY life was unmanageable.

I had not accepted I was powerless over the relationship either. I did not know when enough was enough. In fact, I now realised I was powerless over everything but my own thoughts, my actions, and my behaviour. Yes, I had changed a lot, yet I had not really let go of the relationship with the alcoholic, mentally or emotionally.

I also realised that I had been good at accepting others as they were, but not this man I had lived with. I had accepted my ex-husband to the point of not being able to tolerate the environment around his excessive drinking. I admit this was pretty contradictory, because I too was a drinker. But I could not understand anyone wanting to drink through the week, unless Christmas fell on a weekday or we were on holiday.

The slogan 'Let go and let God' was worn out in my mind, along with the Serenity Prayer. These slogans had been my lifesaver for those past 5-6 years as I sat in meetings while I slowly absorbed the steps.

I could not see how unmanageable my finances had become, even to the stage of taking responsibility for paying my partner's numerous court fines to ensure they were paid. I would even go to court with him to make sure he actually attended.

I smoked cigarettes and cannabis, so my life was pretty unmanageable. And I continued to take my partner back over and over, because it was easier to have him back than to feel emotional pain. It was easier to smoke or eat than to feel. My emotional maturity was around 9-11 years old, but I suspect 11 as the age at which my emotions shut down in some way, due to the distress of losing a stalwart figure in my life – my papa – along with the rite of passage females go through with menstruating.

We talk about feeling lighter, or feeling low and depressed (dark). Positive or negative. Yin or yang. So far, I had given this step plenty of lip service, yet I had not really 'got it' fully into my psyche. I had it on an intellectual level, not an intelligence level. For me, the intellect is the mind, and intelligence is the heart. And I feel that these steps need to be integrated into the heart. The heart needs to drive the vehicle (human body). Most humans are driven by their minds.

So, this took me onto the next step, but first I had to experience how it was for the alcoholic in my life and other alcoholics, their powerlessness with alcohol, and why they continued to drink.

Throughout the book I tend to refer more to alcohol, because this was my main choice of drug. But I have dabbled with other substances over the years, usually to fit in with whoever I was hanging out with. And at that time, I was still around people who took, and continue to take, other classes of substances.

Today, I choose not to be in the company of people who abuse any drugs. That does not mean I will not be in the company of people who take alcohol in social settings. I have not got issues with others who want to take alcohol. I surely did have, yet I have witnessed and experienced both sides of the coin, remember. The good and not good.

Let's go back to the two ladies who were my confidants at the beginning of my journey with the 12 Steps. Let's call them Dora and Elsie. I soon figured that one was positive and the other was, in my humble opinion, quite negative. However, one was living with a sober partner who had attended AA for some years; the other was living with a drinking partner who would often binge. She also had family who would go on drinking sprees. So, I guess they experienced the programme on an intellectual level, too.

Even though they had big hearts, their environments told me that they were what we call 'old school', with those belief systems that you stay in a marriage until 'death do you part' and stick to the 'in sickness and in health' vows. Even to the point of living with total denial of others' behaviours as acceptable.

These two women were really a godsend for me. They accepted me as I was and chose to love me through my dark moments, my denial, and through the good times, too. Elsie would say to me, 'You're ok, Lorna, aren't you?' and I would say 'Yes, but…' She'd reply, 'Yes, but you're actually ok.'

I hated when she said that. I wanted to be more than just ok. It drove me scatty in my mind. I needed to see that the chaos and drama was dwindling in my life, and as an adrenalin junkie being 'ok' just did not cut it for me! I wanted happiness. Bliss. Ecstasy (no, not the substance drug). Just to know what that felt like.

Admitting that I was powerless over people, places, and things, really took me all those years. It was the people part I struggled with. You see, I finally had to own up to being a control freak! Ouch! That hurt. Truth!

I would also find out that this 'ism' would be doing press-ups at the end of my bed, waiting to show itself if I was to not keep guard at the door of my mind. How could I do that? By talking and reasoning things out with others, and by setting in motion a daily practice of meditation. To journal what was going on in my mind. The journalling was easy, as it was something I had done for many years, but this meditation thing was more difficult. However, I was willing to try.

I was starting to see that my 'pain' was in my thinking; that was where it started from. I was told that 'pain is inevitable, suffering is optional'. Aye, but...

I was also told that 'gratitude changes attitude' and started to practise this daily. Even though my life had improved immensely, once I started really studying how others had dealt with this step and put it into practice in their lives, my world started to improve even more. New people were entering, and others were leaving. People from my past were also returning, although I was not really aware of this until later.

These steps were there for me to take at my leisure, yet I felt the years I had already spent sitting in meeting after meeting, convention after convention, coffee chat after coffee chat, were long enough to be hanging around. And I still had an 'ache' I couldn't put my finger on, like a knot in my stomach a lot of the time.

Most of all, I was extremely impatient! I was still mentally attached to the alcoholic in my life; even my ex-husband was still in my life. I so hated to fall out with people and did not want to upset anyone, even though I regularly did. The expression 'if you love them, let them go' took on a new meaning. I thought I had to remain friends with them so as not to upset them.

It is so simple to see, in hindsight, and I sometimes cringe when I look back and realise what my life was like then.

Everything I said I would NEVER get involved with, I got involved with. Weekday drinking, taking other substances, infidelity, incurring heavy debts, self-sabotage through sexual conduct. Even the way I talked to myself was awful. I'd stand at the mirror and say the most awful of things to the face looking back. Then I'd eat more. I think it was only the adrenalin and smoking that kept me relatively slim, along with constantly being on the move.

I was a bit obsessive about my weight, yet other 'things' would take over my thinking and until I dealt with those, the weight issues didn't really show up in my awareness. I had always said I would never tolerate abuse towards me from anyone. But that was a laugh. I was abusing myself, so I attracted that into my life from others, too.

In that year, as it happened, I attended 12 conventions, which paralleled with the 12 Steps I was taking. A friend from the fellowship came with me to nine of these 12, and we would have 'meetings' on the way there and on the way home again. I continued to read up on each step with every piece of literature to hand, and sent my answers at the end of each chapter of each step to Rosemary. (I only got to the third step with her, then I changed sponsors. More on that to come.)

With the first step came a convention in Ireland – the Scottish/Irish Gathering, which I had attended the two previous years. The theme of the convention was 'Taking Care of Ourselves'. The conventions were run by AA with Al Anon participation, so the latter sometimes had their own theme. I hoped that meant I was well on the way to a manageable life by studying and taking the steps with reliable people who had walked this walk before me. This convention always felt like a spring clean for me; a spring clean of my mind. And I believed it was right to take care of the mind and the rest would follow.

So, I finally accepted that I was powerless over alcohol and that my life was unmanageable. The years of meetings, reading literature, the people around me, and the conventions I had attended, had brought me to this point. And while I realised I still had a way to go yet, I could see a Higher Power now leading the way at times, when I would let him/her in.

At this point, I'd like to invite you to find a quiet spot to sit with yourself, and commit to do this for the longest time you can – even if it's only for five minutes. Anyone can find five minutes in a day. I hear plenty say they have no time to meditate, yet they can always find time to go to the toilet! You can even do this exercise then, if you don't have any other time.

There are great phone apps out there to download. Meditate.me is a great one, starting with only 10-minute guided meditations and building up to half an hour. My longest meditation to date has been four hours, but I have friends who have gone way longer than that.

Realise that if you stopped breathing, you would 'die'. Contemplate that. What would that mean? What does death mean for you? Do you believe in God? A Higher Power? Do you believe in love? What are your belief (B) systems (S)? Who taught you to believe what you believe? Are you willing to believe there maybe something bigger than YOU?

Contemplate these questions as you sit quietly for that five minutes. Then commit to making this a regular practice every day, and see what difference it can make to your thinking and your life.

Chapter Five

February 2008

'Insanity: doing the same thing over and over again and expecting different results.'

Albert Einstein

STEP 2: 'Came to believe that a power greater than ourselves could restore us to sanity.'

My birthday was coming up, and I went to my friend's house and embarked on a three-day alcohol-fuelled bender with her, her partner, and a few others. This was AFTER taking Step One. So, I had to FEEL some real powerlessness now, and to have empathy with what it was to maybe walk in another's shoes. To walk in the shoes of an alcoholic, in this case.

On the third day of drinking, I was asked to leave an event I was at because of my behaviour there. I was absolutely mortified about this. Humiliation. It was a sombre occasion with a storyline to music, and I kept clapping my hands and wanting it to be a ceilidh. Folks in the audience were telling me to 'ssshhhhh', but that was like a red rag to a bull to me, and clearly a trigger for me to become vocal! I had no idea then that this all stemmed from deep-rooted fear.

I had always thought the taste of alcohol was pretty disgusting, yet I would take it to fit in and for the effect of being the attention-seeking, spotlight-dodger that I was, and which was amplified when I took alcohol.

After the three days of drinking, the mental torture and the tremors kicked in like I had never experienced in my life before. I was hallucinating, and it was horrendous. I had never ever felt this way or experienced this from drinking before. I knew it had been a long time since I had been drinking for this amount of days, yet somehow I felt that what I was experiencing was different. I could not quite put my finger on it.

Then it dawned on me! I was experiencing how it must be for an alcoholic and their need to keep drinking daily to avoid this terror, and I could now understand how that would and could happen for them. It was not a pretty realisation, but the positive from it was that I grew in compassion for the suffering alcoholic. The suffering human. My mind, body, and spirit were in turmoil, and I realised this was self-harming and self-sabotage to a degree I did not want to experience again. Ever!

But, I questioned myself, if a drinker/alcoholic could stop for a certain amount of time, then why would they want to even lift another drink if they suffered like this? I could not understand this, yet I wanted to. There had been many times in the past when I had gone on a bender myself and sworn off drink, only to do it all over again at some social gathering, like a wedding. I was a Scottish Highlander, for God's sake! It was in my blood. We had to drink! There must be something wrong with you if you didn't drink! It's a known fact that the Scots can drink! Whisky is our heritage!

I knew I needed to continue to attend open AA meetings, as well as my own meetings, because I could identify with both the non-alcoholic and the alcoholic. So, I found out where and when the next conventions would be held, and made up my mind to get to them all.

The 2nd Step came at a convention in Motherwell, with the theme of 'A New Way of Life'. The Al Anon theme at this one was 'From Survival to Recovery', which was one of the first books I had read when I first went to a meeting. The group had a library for anyone to read the literature, and I had bought the daily reads.

One of the daily reads (ODAT= One Day At a Time) had too much emphasis on the God topic for me. It had many Bible quotes, which I hated. But as I 'grew up' emotionally, I began to realise that anything which made me uncomfortable was usually something that eventually would be good for me. Some would say it was a lesson; now I would say it was a gift. And I grew to love this daily read, as the Bible messages changed for me, too. No, I am not religious. I just needed to religiously keep up with instilling new information into my mind to change it.

This 2nd convention was where I met up in person with Rosemary. She and her partner were great convention-goers, and always the first on the dance floor in the evening. She was the same age as my mother.

At a previous convention, I had been asked to do a top table, where we share our own story and experience with the view that it can help someone else. I had been a total wreck before doing it, but it felt good afterwards as a lot of things do when we have faced a fear. I was told that to do a top table would enhance my 'growth' within the programme, and looking back, that definitely was the case.

At one meeting, I met another woman who 'told my story' from a top table one night, and I sat crying. The first part of her story did not resonate with me, but when she talked about her relationship with her alcoholic partner...

ping! My ears shot open. I felt as though she was talking about me and my partner. We had very similar stories, but she had ended her relationship.

I felt as though she had what I wanted at that time, so I made a point of going outside to chat with her later, as we were both smokers. We hit it off, exchanged phone numbers, and this was the start of another soul mate relationship. Soul sisters.

She was near my age in years and, once we compared our stories, we had so many similarities it was uncanny. It helped me immensely in knowing I could end the mental relationship with my partner through this woman's story and experience. Her alcoholic was her wee lad's dad, so he was still very much in her life although they were no longer living together. Yet they were on and off – just as in my situation.

She and I were both smokers of cannabis, and when I travelled down to stay with her, we would puff away on an evening once her wee boy was asleep and her other kids were out or away with their dad for the weekend. Her ex was still smoking this drug, too, yet I never met him when he was under the influence of alcohol or cannabis. He would eventually hit alcohol again as his chosen choice of drug.

Sadly, he could not recover from this horrible dis-ease, and eventually it took his life. People often say that someone died due to liver failure or cancer of the throat, but they very seldom say someone died from the dis-ease of alcoholism.

A man from my village was told if he did not stop drinking, his stomach might burst. And it did. At his funeral, the minister announced that he had died from alcoholism, and some of the locals were absolutely fuming. They were squirming in their seats. But why? Do you think it was showing them something within themselves that they did not want to see? The poor man's stomach had burst, how dare the minister tell a lie like he did?! Denial?

I started to notice that as I was taking these 'steps', my life was improving both inwardly and outwardly. I suppose life had started to improve from the very first meeting, yet it was taking me some time to absorb the depth of the programme and the severe mental trauma I had endured. When I say 'inwardly', I mean a peace was settling.

I also noticed that I would feel amazing while studying these steps. Even though we, as a group, had shared our views around the steps, to delve into studying them felt different. This was a new level of recovery. Recovery from a hopeless place within.

My biggest battle has always been with my thinking. And even though I was clearly much more aware of myself and my thinking, somewhere within me I still felt I could sort it myself (ISM for me now meant I'll Sort it Myself). I was learning lots of new quotes and little ditties when I was going to conventions or other meetings, and would often return to my home group and spout them to everyone. One member called me 'Queen of the Quotes'. Of course, my ego mind loved this.

I should like to say that alcoholism is still very much around me, and I see it being played out within family members and friends. Remember, you do not have to drink to suffer from alcoholism. When stuck in denial, though, we cannot see it.

I can recall a time when I had been asking someone about the Higher Power and the 2nd step. I'd commented, 'If a Higher Power restores us to sanity, doesn't that mean we are insane?' In reply, one lady had asked me how my

behaviour was. Oh! Another revelation. My behaviour was not the best; in fact, it was horrendous at times; it was insane behaviour a lot of the time. If insanity is doing the same things and expecting different results, I was a master at it. It is also said that a problem cannot be resolved with the same head that caused it in the first place. So, it was taking some time to change my mind, I realised.

Guilt came back again. Deeper shame came at the back of it. And shame is worse than guilt to deal with. Drinking was the solution to deeper issues, but it then becomes harder to stop through the mental obsession. What a merry-go-round!

I experienced guilt over my behaviour around my children and family. Guilt about my behaviour in my marriage. Guilt at my behaviour as a teenager towards my parents, especially my mam. I felt totally overwhelmed with it.

Thank God I had people around me to walk me through that guilt, as I was feeling so depressed with it. Again, I was keeping my feelings all on the inside, and only sharing my vulnerability with my Al Anon family.

There had to be a loving God, right? Or was this depression part of a punishment from the God that I understood? I was still not getting this God malarkey! More and more questions were coming than were being answered. One day I believed, the next I didn't… then I would feel guilty. It was like being in the bath as a kid and trying to catch the soap bar. Sometimes you would catch it, other times it would slip through your hands. This is what it felt like to believe in a Higher Power for me.

Again, the past would come forward in the quiet meditative/contemplative times I set aside for this 'work'. I knew the meetings were about sharing our experience, strength, and hope. And this step held out the hand of hope to me.

I was beating myself up with such a big metaphorical stick; I felt I deserved to be punished. A victim. But it had become easier for me to call people when I felt the mental chaos erupt within my mind, and other members would tell me off for being too hard on myself. They'd encourage me to be gentle with myself while walking this walk.

I was learning compassion. Compassion for the suffering alcoholic, for my own suffering, and for humanity's suffering. Use of substances was a way of avoiding the suffering to a degree, but afterwards, one would have to keep using to get over the feelings that followed.

Deep within me I had this loathing, and the people who had walked this walk knew that and loved me without judgment. My friends and family could not do that, as they did not understand me now. And when I was apologising for being such a bad family member or friend, I was met with a diversity of opinions.

In Step 1, I had admitted (and accepted) that I was powerless over everything except my own thoughts, actions, and behaviours. Yet my thoughts towards myself were horrendous. Now I realised I was making my thoughts my Higher Power; they would take over my waking hours, and it was the meditation times which were my saving grace. The meditation was related to Step 11, so I was being prepared even at this point.

So, the programme had become my temporary Higher Power until I came to believe through changing my thinking patterns and behaviours, meditation, and aiming to make amends to others. I was also God shopping. By God shopping, I mean I went to various churches to seek out this Higher Power I understood as God.

I went to a Catholic baptism, understood the way the priest talked, and remember thinking I liked it. I even

went to visit the local priest and got a book on converting to Catholicism. I think it is still in the loft!

I was also learning that 'this too shall pass' meant the good and the not so good. Everything passes; even the soul from the human body passes. In 2005, my dear dad became ill, and I questioned God then and asked 'why?' Yet if there was not a power that was loving in its essence, how did I manage to resolve a relationship with my dad that made it easier to accept his leaving the planet than it would have prior Al Anon?

Dad never knew what I was really doing; he was just happy that I was doing it. I overheard him saying to someone, 'Och, she's in that alcoholics anonymous thing and she's got her drinking under control now.' I gave a wee smile as I realised I did not want to correct him that it was not AA I belonged to. This programme and the people in it held me and supported me through my many days of crazy thinking.

I had always been very trusting of people. I remember my mam saying to me when I was a teen, 'You'll end up in bother, Lorna, because you take everyone at face value.' Of course, she was right, although she was very off in another way!

My parents always tried to protect me from the 'big bad world', as Dad called it. I believe they fell into the negative aspects of the world and fed this to me, which filled me with a great fear. I filed this belief to take out whenever I left that wee village. And I would run home to them any chance I got, because I could not cope in the world.

I made everything and everybody my 'god' throughout my life. First of all, my mother and my gran, my papa and my dad. Then my best friend. Then Bettyhill. Then the things I accumulated from others. I would hold onto them.

I wasn't a hoarder, yet I did find it difficult to let go. People, places, and things had been my god... or goddesses. Everything that helped me to feel good was only temporary. A new pair of Dr Martin boots, a leather coat, a nice haircut. A cigarette after a meal. Oh, how I loved that fag!

Due to my churching as a child, the God I had within me was one who would dish out punishment if I was a 'bad girl'. I recall having to recite, while holding my right hand up, 'Hand up to God and hope to die if I tell a lie.' Wow! That is very scary to a child, and if an adult told me to do something and I rebelled, I was that bad girl. A brat.

I witnessed men of the cloth hitting children for blasphemy. And I would be told off myself for 'taking the Lord's name in vain' whenever I wailed, 'oh, good God!' or 'for God's sake'. I thought I could get away with saying it in Gaelic. Not a chance! But I was just repeating what I heard, so why was it okay for the adults to curse yet not me?

I got married in a church and I wanted my daughter christened in a church, because that's what I believed you did. But I fell out with the minister when he told me what I had to do for that to happen. He actually called me a liar about who my local minister was. I was living in Yorkshire at the time, within a military environment, so when he said I had to become a church member and pay money to the church each month before he would christen my daughter, I ran home to Mam to sort him out!

That was me – a married woman with a child, running home to Mammy to sort out a discussion that she could not hold herself, as it would mean a confrontation of a sort. She did go and tell him what she thought of him, and that was when I left the church. Of course, as the years went on and anything went wrong for me, I believed that I had to accept this 'punishment' because I did not go to church. More BS!

Always this God was mentioned, and I was terrified of 'IT'; whatever 'IT' was. As a child, I had asked why I had to have polished shoes for church, and why I needed to be 'dressed up' when Jesus wore old robes and sandals. I was told I needed to be seen and not heard. This, I must state, was not from my immediate family but from others.

In my group it was suggested that I should 'act as if' there was a Higher Power. To use time in nature to notice and ask questions. To become more aware of when I may think a Higher Power might be at work in my life. So, I kept praying, talking to this God, and meditating, waiting for the answer. Or I would start to notice things people might say, or something I'd read or heard in a movie that stood out to me. I started to believe this was a Higher Power 'talking' to me through other avenues, through other people, places, and things.

Nature was showing me how we as humans are so intricately woven into the tapestry of the seasons and the weather and the moods of nature. I really started to see the beauty in the Highlands for the first time, and to ask who created this. I was practising gratitude for being brought up in this part of the world, with wonderful scenery, fresh air to breathe to bring joy to the heart, the oceans with their changing moods and colours, memories of childhood frolicking on the golden sands, with purple heather underfoot, and rolling in the hay fields throughout the summer holidays.

I realised that everywhere I had lived actually had something special, and it was me that was unhappy. My world was as I saw and believed it to be. In the same way that I saw and believed I was – ugly, and unwelcoming, and unsafe.

It was really good fun to be noticing the beauty, and I remembered the ceilidhs when my papa would sing Gaelic songs and play the chanter, how I loved to sneak in with the adults on their get-togethers, visiting my godmother who lived at the American Naval base 30 miles away and telling my friends at school I'd been to America.

It had not been a bad childhood. I was loved, very much loved. Yet I had made a lot of these people my Higher Power because I believed they all knew what was best for me... because they told me they did.

Now, though, I was gaining trust. I started to go to the Spiritual Church, and I quite liked it and the people there. This was more 'my thing'. No-one coming to try to save me or let me know that I was a sinner!

Then, through my work of supporting the vulnerable, I had to take a service user to church, because that is what his family wanted for him. It was great, because I was there in a work capacity and not because I wanted to go. Yet there was something about this church I liked. It wasn't how I remembered church. As kids, we were given strict instructions to 'behave' and 'be quiet' in church, and given Pan Drop sweets to shut us up. But the children in this church were running around freely, then they went off with helpers to their Sunday school for a part of the service. It was really refreshing to see the kids so happy, and everyone seemed friendly.

I still had this idea that God was outside of me, and that I would only find 'Him' in a church. How naïve was I?

The word 'consciousness' was appearing in some other literature I was reading, but I kept going back to my Al Anon books and monthly magazines. I still had a long way to go, but I kept using the Serenity prayer regularly. 'God, grant me serenity, to accept the things I cannot change, courage to change the things I can, and the wisdom to know the difference.' I adored this prayer and I would use the first two lines... a lot!

More and more I was realising my experiences were occurring due to the thoughts I was having. BeLIEf systems that were instilled from childhood.

So, I asked God to lead me, to guide me every morning, and I would journal my new thoughts. I found this little prayer I liked: 'God, take me where you want me to go. Let me meet who you want me to meet. Let me say what you want me to say, and keep ME out of your way!'

My awareness had expanded due to the 'study of these steps', because 'they're essential to progress'. I was now taking them more seriously, so my awareness was expanding. New people would pop in with 'messages' which I would finally hear and take on board. All this was helping me to 'come to believe' in a new way, with an opening of my heart. I just had to learn to trust in this Higher Power and call it what I wanted. I called 'It' Higher Power and then moved onto the Universe as I started to look at what this consciousness was/is.

There were plenty of moments of clarity where I could now see 'something' must surely have been looking after me in my past. Protecting me.

I'd like to share a 'God' story with you to illustrate my point.

Some years later, I took up running, and went to Stornoway for a half marathon. Long before we went, I asked my partner if we would stay at the caravan park in the bunkhouse because we were on a budget plan. He agreed, yet 'something' deep within me was saying he wouldn't like that. I phoned and booked anyway, and as it grew closer to the time to go, I kept asking if he was sure he wanted to stay there. He'd nod his head, but I still had this 'feeling' that he didn't really want to.

On the day of the trip, the ferry was running late. As we were docking, my partner turned to me and said, 'Och, let's see if we can get a hotel.' And a domestic ensued! I was really annoyed that he'd pulled this out of the bag at the last minute, without having the decency to let the folks at the caravan park know. I felt it was rude to phone at this late stage to say we were not coming, but I told him he could phone... and he refused.

Long story short. We got a lovely hotel, everyone was friendly, and it was so comfortable that I forgot about the caravan park. I was always nervous on the night before an event like this, and on the morning of the race I would always pray for a running angel to keep me inspired. The phone buzzed with a message; it was the caravan park asking if we still needed the bunkhouse. I panicked and text a reply back to them saying, 'No, not coming, family issues at home'.

I did not feel good about lying, but tried not to think about it and headed off to the race! BANG! The starting gun went off and I tripped and fell flat on my face! Now... you could say it was a punishment from God for lying, depending on your beliefs. Yet I didn't feel that way. As far as I was concerned, it was just an unfortunate fall, and although my elbows and knees were bleeding, I continued to run. It felt like a good excuse not to try to keep up with anyone else.

People could clearly see blood running from my elbows and knees, so that allowed me to become the child and milk their sympathy! Then at around the 3-4 miles mark, I was alongside a tall, handsome man who looked like he was out for a country stroll. Here was me, puffing and sweating, already knackered, and my head doing a number on me about having another 10 miles to go.

When I told this man that he looked so relaxed, he replied, 'I usually pray to God at times like that.' BOOM! Here was my running angel, I thought. When I told him that, he laughed and said he was quite happy to run with me because he had done it many times before, so it was just a stroll for him. I felt his sincerity and settled into a plod!

Then he said, 'So, my name is Gordon, what's yours?'

'Lorna.'

'Lorna, where do you come from?'

'I live in Inverness, but come from Bettyhill. Do you know it?'

'Not really,' he said.

I explained where it was, and then I asked, 'What about you? Are you local?'

'Yes,' he replied, 'I own the caravan park.'

Holy shit! In that moment, I swear I heard a voice inside me laughing loudly. I just remember looking to the heavens and saying to myself, You're having a fucking laugh! Out of 150 entrants in this race, I had to end up with the owner of the caravan park whom I had lied to in a text message. And there could not be many Lornas from Inverness running in this event. Immediately, I imagined reaching the finishing line and putting my hands around Robert's neck to throttle him. Blame.

I actually started to pick up speed and left him without saying anything. I forgot about my bloody body, and speed, and everything, as I was consumed with my lie and how I could make amends and get out of feeling so guilty and bad.

At around 10 miles, we started on an incline and I could sense Gordon not far behind me. I knew he would come up beside me again, because I just could not go faster at that point. As he approached, he called, 'You're doing great, Lorna. Nine-and-a-half minute miles.'

Oh, really? I thought. Don't think I've managed THAT before! With that, I turned to him and told him, blurting out how sorry I was, and explaining what had happened. To my surprise, he burst out laughing, saying it was really ok, how he loved to see God at work every day and this was one of those moments. He was so bloody lovely and kind that I felt even worse!

He assured me all was well, and he would run the rest of the way with me. He was actually a religious man, and we had a great blether the rest of the way to the finish line where Robert, as usual, was waiting for me. When I introduced him to Gordon, his face was a picture!

I'm forever grateful to this man for showing me such kindness and helping me get the best time to date for a half marathon! So, I always say, if you don't believe in God, you will when I tell you this story! It confirms for me the inner God who has a sense of humour. Not the punishing type at all.

After all these years, this was confirmation for me that I had 'come to believe in a power greater than myself' and 'IT' was living and breathing within and without. A living 'IT' within everyone and everything. You can take a cup of salt water from the sea, but it is still a part of the ocean. We are still a part of a living Consciousness (Energy) we mainly call God! What a revelation!

Chapter Six
March 2008

'Man says, Show me and I'll trust you... God says,
Trust me and I'll show you.'
Psalm 1266

STEP 3: 'Made a decision to hand my will and my life
over to the care of God as I understand Him.'

In Al Anon, we were told of the 3 Cs of alcoholism: we did not Cause it; we could not Control it; nor Cure it. We also had the 3 As in there: Awareness, Acceptance, and Action.

I was aware that this programme was for ME and not for the people around me or those in my life who I proclaimed caused me bother. And I was also becoming more aware of myself. Accepting all this new thinking into my life was like learning a new language, and my daughters would remind me at times when I fell into old patterns. They would joke that I was part of a cult, but I was conscious that my life was better, and how it was continuously changing the more I continued to practise these steps and principles. The saying 'the proof is in the pudding' comes to mind. I could not always notice the changes myself, but people around me within the programme would point things out to me, and my journals showed me how much I was changing.

I was now starting to see that perhaps the God of my understanding had not left me; I had left Him, or Her, or whatever I perceived IT to be. I knew that I had to find this Higher Power to hand my issues over to, because I usually made a mess of things whenever I tried to figure out shit by myself. But how could I know if I was handing it over?

I started to become aware of my gut and the responses it made. I had a friend who did not understand what I was doing, and she maintained it was a bullshit way to get out of dealing with issues. We agreed to disagree.

I became willing, and that was all that was being asked of me. When I over-thought things – which was a lot – I would feel overwhelmed with life. I had a habit of gathering as much information as I could and then making decisions by phoning people I knew who would just listen, and sometimes challenge me, so that I could make the right choices for me and those around me. I still found it hard to do this on my own and be happy with my decisions.

It was beginning to dawn on me that I had allowed others to make decisions for me throughout my whole life, even when I did not want them to. For instance, when I decided to leave my marriage, I was sent a five-page letter by a family member, asking me if I knew what I was doing!!! All the pressure from others' opinions, along with a few other factors, then convinced me to change my mind and stay longer in the marriage than I wanted to.

I realised I had become an actress of sorts. A people-pleaser to get others to like me, because I was actually scared of what people thought about me and what they would say. I felt I had to be like them to be liked. I have since learned that there are many of us out there who feel the same way, but the Steps were now challenging me to look within myself. Through this fellowship, I was meeting many new people from many different places, and I was immersed in this programme of recovery.

Trying to discern what my HP (Higher Power) wanted from me, and what Lorna wanted, started to become easier. At one convention, I bought a book which was on sale there and couldn't wait to get back to read it. But when I sat down that night with the book, I just could not get into it. That was when I realised that books would show up when I was ready to read them; if I was not ready, I would not be able to start with them.

And I'm still like that with books. I have so many sitting on the shelves with markers in them or which have not even been started. But now I trust that if I am to read them, then I shall. One particular book, called Opening Our Hearts and Transforming Our Losses – a Conference Approved Literature (CAL) – really resonated with me in its last pages. As with most CAL, it's full of members' sharings, and I just knew then that I was really ready to end the relationship with my then partner. You know when you just know something? Well, that was the book that sealed the deal!

From a young age, we are taught to look after others, and even when I was really suffering mentally within this programme, it was suggested to me to go and help someone else. Helping another for me involves listening to them, offering guidance via suggestions – rather than advice or my opinions – and allowing them to make decisions for themselves.

This step asked me to make a decision, so I might as well. It was said that there were three frogs on a lily pad. Two jumped off, and the third made the decision to jump. It did not mean it would jump. This analogy made it easier for me to make the decision and become willing to hand my will over to this Higher Power. Let's face it. My will had caused me to arrive at the point of wanting to die, so this had to be better.

I used the daily reads to try to figure out my feelings and give them names. Courage, selfishness, fear, hostility, aggressiveness, happy, excited, nervous, etc. I was putting the study time in and reading every piece I could find around this step, mainly from others who had walked before me. But there were so many contradictions.

In the end, I took what I liked and left the rest: 'Thy Will be done, not mine.' I decided I would ask my HP to help me with 'Its' will for me for that day, and began to allow a small prayer book to open randomly at a page. I started to notice that my day would fall around that prayer. In fact, my intuition could usually let me know in advance how it would pan out if I didn't adhere to the check-ins with my HP; sometimes on an hourly basis. I did it with an urgency!

Some days, I hated it all and I would stomp around like a spoilt child, wishing some pack of marauding wolves would eat me up when I looked at my behaviour! But on the whole, it strengthened my relationship with my HP. Yet I still fought trust. I could not figure out when I had learned not to trust my own gut feelings, even if my intuition did give me advanced signals. So, I was told to look at where I tripped, not where I fell.

It soon dawned on me that I had needed to survive my emotions. I was addicted to thinking; Was there a 12 Step programme on emotions anonymous? Actually, yes, there was one. Not here, though. Then I wondered if there was a group for over-thinking. I was even willing to start up a group! Oh, help! Was I going mad again? Was I becoming addicted to this programme?

My new sponsor, Angie, had introduced me to Reiki, which is an ancient energy healing modality. When she asked if I fancied being attuned to this modality, initially I refused, but two months later I was heading to Stirling through a synchronistic event to do my Level 1 Reiki!

Some people might call it a coincidence (or a God-incident!), but I don't feel there are any in the Universe! I also signed up for a Complementary Therapies course that year. I had journalled at one stage: 'Please, if there is a God, let me have another chance at this thing called Life and I'll agree to let YOU guide me.' I realise I was probably bargaining with the HP, but lo and behold I was going back to education. Back to school, if you like. But this time I was going because I had found something I was interested in, so I was making choices for myself and not for anyone else. Angie decided to do the same, and she too signed up for college, even though we lived hundreds of miles apart.

I now found myself being introduced to books that came under the bracket of self-development or self-help, and picking up pieces of myself through them. They included, Women Who Love Too Much (When You Keep Wishing & Hoping He'll Change) by Robin Norwood, and Co-Dependency No More, Beyond Co-Dependency, and The Language of Letting Go, all by Melody Beattie.

These books began to open me up in a new way. Again, I identified with them all and highlighted paragraphs and pages that resonated with me, finally realising that I was co-dependent and had not known it. I still studied my Al Anon daily reads and kept journalling, and I was starting to see the relevance of how the steps ran from one to the next.

It was becoming clearer to me that I was powerless over others and their decisions and actions. My life had become unmanageable due to my own insane behaviour, which had picked up momentum over the decades due to the choices I had made. I also noticed how I was still trying to fix others, attempting to get people I knew to come along to meetings. Of course, this was because I was changing and starting to notice these traits in the people in my life.

I was still looking outwards more than inwards, though, and I was hurting badly on days when I would recognise that my own thinking was wayward. My initial reaction would be to scream at others to 'fuck off!', then I would feel so bad because of it and have to go apologise. This really drained my energy.

I had to journal for the Reiki Level 1 course, along with being invited to do a 21-day cleanse to eliminate from the body anything that does not serve it. I believe that was the start of cleaning the inside at a deeper level, and I noticed that the smell of smoke began to really repulse me.

The thought of practising complementary therapies with people and working with them around health did not sit well with me smoking. So, I knew I would have to give up. After several attempts, I finally stopped with the help of cessation. A week after taking a small tab under my tongue, I thought, What the hell? May as well go cold turkey again. So, I did. The nurse said I had a strong habit; I say I had an addiction. I searched online to see what came up:

According to the website, **Difference Between**, 'Habit is a behaviour pattern developed by frequent repetition of the act over and over to the point the brain does it automatically. An addiction is a compulsive need of a certain thing or substance to the body, which when deprived causes horrible effects. A habit can be controlled or modified, while addiction cannot be controlled and requires professional help for modification.'

That referred to smoking, and I like how it says, 'while addiction cannot be controlled and requires professional help for modification'. This tells me that a professional can help, whereas most of the people I encountered in the 12 Step Programme had tried that route, yet no human power could help them modify the use of substances of any kind. Only a Higher Power could do that.

Let's look back at the first three steps of this programme in their simplest form: I can't. He can. I'll let Him. Sounds easy, eh? No. Practice, practice, and even more practice. You see, if I had gone in right away to practise these steps when I first 'got them', I doubt I would have stuck it out. The deep conditioning from childhood, growing until I was 39 years, was embedded in me; it was not going to shift in one sitting. Not even in the first six meetings.

Bill Wilson described the 12 Steps as a bridge to normal living. Ok, so I wanted to cross that bridge. Study of the steps and putting the practice into daily living were proving to me that normal living was achievable. That meant to have peace in the home. But the peace had to come from me. I had three teenage daughters, so I had to change things to show them there could be a different way. If I was learning that early childhood (and before) was where we learned how to 'do life', then they had to be affected, too. Unfortunately, the older two left home while I was still in recovery, so I feel they never got to experience the totality of this 'new Mam' back then.

I had to learn to ask for help before coming to the point of playing the martyr, as I now realised that is what I had always done in the past. I was also guilty of trying to take others' responsibilities on for them. So, to now be able to hand others over to their Higher Powers through prayer, was truly liberating.

I still reached the point of drama within my mind before asking for help on occasions, but the three steps were designed to stop me from doing that and I knew life would become simpler because of them. I would use the slogan H.A.L.T., which meant Hungry? Angry? Lonely? Tired? It was suggested if I was all of these, I could phone someone and meet for a bite to eat, talk my anger out, and then have a nap afterwards.

Sometimes, I felt as though I would never master these steps. But thankfully, I had people at the end of a phone who, by the grace of God, would respond to my pleas for help. The more awareness I gained, the more my HP would put people, places, and things into my awareness to help me.

Of course, being human means I can still react, but then I have to make amends for that and offer humble apologies. I was beginning to learn that I did not need the approval of anyone except myself. Until that stage, I had based my life on needing to have others' approval to show me that I was ok, and I had always judged my accomplishments on others' opinions.

Until the day I set foot on a spiritual path, my life's beLIEf system had been that I must get a good education if I was to have a decent job, then work all the hours to get money, to be successful and to find a husband to take care of – although he would be the main person in the relationship – and for us to have babies. This was honestly what I thought I had to do. The job I would get would set me up until I retired, got a pension, and became 'too old' to do certain things. So, I better make a bloody good go of it, and then I'd die! These were the basic beLIEfs, yet I knew them to be crap!

I now recognise that I have an inner authority which will tell me when I need to eat, or if I am thirsty, or need to go to the toilet, or if I am tired and need to sleep. Yes, an inner authority, not some clock telling me I must go to bed or eat at a specific time.

I had heard all about outer space, yet never about inner space. This was where the inner power resided, so was that the Higher Power? Well, since I tuned into it, my life has certainly run more smoothly and simply. I reckon this Higher Power is also the outer authority, so whatever is happening inside can manifest outside. Many self-help books in the outer space lead you to that place.

Many others have found their truth from the stimulations of societal systems of governments and hierarchy by living lives of simplicity, by getting out in nature and observing their thoughts. I may as well try that, too.

So, when my life feels unmanageable, I can usually realise very quickly that I am distracted by outside influences. Awareness is 90% of the solution, then ask for help. As quick as saying one, two, three. I can't; She can; I'll let Her!

I had taken my third step! The 3rd convention that went with this step was on my home turf in Inverness, where the Al Anon theme was 'Awareness, Acceptance, Action'. The 3 As, as mentioned earlier.

Then one night, sitting on my sofa, I had an amazing experience. I was in such a place of gratitude about how my life was changing. I had soft pan pipe music playing in the background, candles burning… and then it happened!

I had an urge to get my journal and start writing, but it is so hard to explain what occurred in those moments; it was an experience that I can't do justice to with words. At the time, I felt as though I was dying. The pain in my heart was immense, and I had my left hand holding my chest while my right hand kept writing. 'I' was watching this scene unfold from just outside of my body, while simultaneously feeling this tremendous physical pain running through from my heart and feeling blind panic. The other side of my body was working away by writing about the experience in the best way it could, all the while with 'me' watching everything unfold! From that vantage point, I had a massive view of everything unravelling before me as I felt an incredible love overwhelm my whole being!

I knew in that moment how 'God' felt! The tears came then, as grace and tremendous peace filled my being. I felt like I was going to die, yet how could that be when I was being born? Incredible. My body is reacting to the memory even as I write this.

When Rosemary later read what I had written about the experience, she told me that it was a re-birth. She asked if I had read The Moth and the Flame (by Arran Stephens), and I admitted I had only managed 23 chapters because I really didn't understand a lot of it. Rosemary suggested I go back and try reading it again, as she believed I would 'get it' this time. And she was right! The mother of the author had undergone a similar experience, and I have since learned of many other people who have, too. I call it another one of my 'God' moments.

The next day, I woke wondering what had happened. I was still in a place of wonderful peace and love for all sentient beings, and it took me over 10 minutes to get into my car, because I could not believe I had never seen the wonder of this world before. The green grass, the colours of the sky, the clouds, the flowers and trees. I was crying with the wonder of it. I was in LOVE! I never wanted to leave this place.

The feeling slowly faded away as the day progressed, and I discovered that Rosemary was the only person who fully understood what I was talking about. Dear Angie tried to understand, but couldn't. So, I kept very quiet about it, as

I realised the way I would have to describe it would make others think I was barking mad and needed to be certified. It would be another few years before I would meet others who had had similar crazy experiences.

Chapter Seven
April 2008

'Faith is taking the first step, even when you don't see the whole staircase.'
Dr Martin Luther King

STEP 4: 'Made a searching and fearless moral inventory of ourselves.'

Thank God we don't see the whole staircase, because many will not climb it at this step, which is recognised as being the hardest one of all. So, I surrendered this to my Higher Power at this point and decided that it would take however long it would take to visit this step. Some get to this stage and leave any 12 Step Programme. It's too painful.

By that stage, I was beginning to recognise what had my name on it and what didn't, so I did not need to engage in any given situation if I did not want to. However, this seemed to piss some people off and I slowly started to drift from them. One night, I had a dream of this happening. With love, I watched them all drift down from clouds into the sea and lie with their arms crossed over their chests on the seabed, and I knew this was our friendships put to rest in a lovely place.

I felt that God's will was/is just to be kind to myself and others, and to accept others as they are. But even now that can still be difficult to do. I continue to practise this, and sometimes I succeed, other times I don't. Of course, others see this as me being selfish; I see it as making self-caring choices. Perceptions.

The amazing experience on the sofa proved to be the real beginning of change within me. But the outer world had changed, too. I stopped watching TV all the time, as my eldest daughters (aged 21 and 19) were no longer home and my youngest tended to retreat to her room when she was at home. At the age of 17, she spent a lot of time out with her friends, and we were like ships passing in the night. But we enjoyed a good relationship most of the time then, as she was liking this 'new Mam'.

The other two kept in touch via Bebo (before Facebook), which was a social network for teens. The eldest was travelling in Australia; the middle one was in the Army and had gone to Afghanistan for a tour of six months. When folks asked if I was terribly worried about her, I had to give the question some thought, but came to the conclusion I was ok about it because I knew where she was. I was also aware that if anything was to happen, I would soon know, whereas I had no idea where my eldest was unless she got in touch. As she was travelling around a lot, that was more of a worry. Reiki taught me that 'just for today, I will not worry'.

I was not interested in changes in technology and did not even want a mobile phone. I felt as though each day was a new start while travelling this road with the Steps, but realised I was also stepping into hurt as I was healing. It was a rollercoaster of emotions and revelations, yet nothing like the rollercoaster life I had lived before.

This particular step is classed as the hardest of the 12 because it involves us having to delve deep into our own behaviours to make that thorough inventory. At that stage, I had no idea who Lorna was, so I had to re-invent her.

I would like to share with you my life until 2010, because it was part of my inventory. This is how I viewed it.

1970

We moved down to the Highland capital of Inverness when I was aged seven, and I hated it to begin with but eventually settled. It was four-and-a-half hours away from 'home' and my dear grandparents and friends, and this was my first experience of home sickness that I remember. It was also traumatic for me because I was put back a class in my new school. I was also angry because I had to wear a uniform, but did not want to look like other kids. It also meant wearing a skirt! Yuk! I hated skirts. I would carry it in my schoolbag then change in the toilets, because I preferred my jeans.

We girls had to wear navy blue pants and a white top, while boys wore shorts and white vests. How very uncool!

My mother wanted me to learn a musical instrument, but I was aware that the kids that did this were ridiculed. They were the children who spoke better through having elocution lessons, and weren't liked by the kids I warmed to. I actually liked the 'swots' too, though. This is where I really learned to follow others, and I fell into friendship with whoever would like me – usually the ones who happily took sweets from me.

It is also where I began to recognise how adults would compare children – 'So-and-so is doing so well, why can't you be like her?' This, we now know, is detrimental to children's welfare and for many is criticism at its worst. All this before the label of Highly Sensitive Person (HSP) came about. (Another great book worth reading is The

Highly Sensitive Person, How to Thrive When the World Overwhelms You by Elaine Aron, who also wrote The Highly Sensitive Child.)

I had always been classed as 'a big girl', due to being a lot taller than others of my age. I now know expectations were put upon me because of this. Have you noticed how adults tend to talk to kids like they're adults?

I grew to like the school, although I was still always extremely upset when leaving 'home' after a visit. I would go to my aunt's house near Glasgow for the summer holidays, then travel back up North with them, with their trusty caravan towed on the back.

I had a busy and good childhood, with all the luck of living in a town and the country. The joy and freedom of the fresh air from the ocean, golden beaches and hills, lochs and mountains. There were also exciting things to do in the town (which is now a city), like swimming all year round, ice skating, and the shows (fairground) in the summer months. The circus would also come to town, and I could daydream of running away with them. I believe a lot of children felt this way, but don't know what it was that attracted us all then to want a gypsy life on the road.

1975

My mother became pregnant when I was aged 12, and to my delight we moved back 'home' again for me to start in secondary school. I had made good friends in Inverness, whom I loved to write to – although that's a dying art these days.

I was obsessed with the Bay City Rollers – a Scottish boy band who were about as popular as the Beatles had been. Screaming young women would throw themselves at these lads, and oh how I wanted to do that! Fantasy thoughts kept me busy!

The great thing about starting secondary school back at home was there was no uniform! Yay. No rules there!

I became a big sister twice within about four years, and was delighted with my new siblings. Yet I have discovered that this was most likely the age where I stopped 'growing' physically. Between age 13-15. I had already dwindled with my emotional state at age nine, and this was to impact me later in life. The two emotional traumas I mentioned previously, at the age of 11, had played a big part due to my parents having their own issues going on. The spiritual had happened years before that; the physical and mental had yet to come.

My first sister was born a few months before I was to become a teenager, and my second on my 15th birthday.

It was a period when a lot of young girls were falling pregnant in the nearest town of Thurso, and I recall the Scottish newspaper, The Daily Record, carrying the front page declaring, 'The Town of the Gym Slip Mums' with a picture of a schoolgirl with her back to the camera. We all knew who she was at that time; it didn't matter that she had her back to us.

My dad worked away from the village to make decent money, and Mam had me and then two wee ones to contend with. I was a stroppy hormonal teenager with a lot going on emotionally, and I feel she couldn't give me the attention I craved, so I was always running between her and my gran. I was also happy-go-lucky, though. My best friend lived next door to my gran and, as we had been inseparable until we moved, I would hang out at her house or with my other friends in other villages. We were a community of family, and everyone would muck in at certain times of the year like when peat-cutting time came around. We would go to whoever had peat being cut, take a picnic, and spend the day there. Even the weather seemed to be predictable; summer meant the sun shone most days for a period of several months. These are my memories.

I started to dabble with alcohol and boys, pretty much in that order really. Until then, I had loved to hang out at my aunt's; she had a couple of horses. But then even they got put to the side.

1979

I left school and started in college and really felt quite happy, even though I hated the course I was doing. I had a good bunch of friends – one in particular who became a bestie, and we would drink together at the weekends. I lived for Fridays, and on Mondays we would start planning for the weekend all over again. Life was pretty much ok with no major dramas at this point. I even remember reading a problem page in my mother's magazine and laughing because I couldn't understand why people had problems! Then, at the age of 16, I fell in love! Or so I thought!

The 80s

I got engaged, yet my emotional rawness ruled my life; so the relationship ended. I then had what I guess you would call a few 'flings', and finally hooked up with a man I'd lived next door to as a toddler, and we married in 1985. We were too young, and married for all the wrong reasons. He was in the Forces, so we moved a couple of times, initially starting out in Germany, coming back to the UK, then ending up in Germany again.

We both liked to drink, but I noticed that he would drink on weekdays and the weekends, which seemed odd to me. I thought you only drank alcohol at the weekends, after a hard week of work. That had been my teachings.

We would become quite verbally aggressive towards each other, and my temper became worse as my neurosis (a relatively mild mental illness) grew! I reacted.

I was not happy. We had three daughters, but we were both too emotionally immature to have a grown-up discussion about personal feelings. And we were ill-equipped to help our daughters with their emotions. I even studied his upbringing to help me come to compassion for him and his childhood. I knew his parents from the village.

With a busy home, and three daughters under the age of five at one stage, I stopped journalling so much and fell into fantasy for the second time since childhood. I would visualise myself with one of the celebs who were around then, like the actor Brad Pitt, and built up obsessions in my mind. The scenarios I was imagining were far-fetched but kept me functioning and looking ok to the outside world. I could not find a nice balance in my way of responding in and to life, and was pretty harem-scarem to folks. I learned later in life that some people were actually scared of me. I believe that was due to my reactive personality and not being able to control my emotions.

I picked up many more masks to suit occasions that I found myself in, and built layer upon layer of a F#cked up, Insecure, Neurotic & Emotional person (F.I.N.E). Unfortunately, I did not realise that I was already in victimhood and insanity!

The 90s-00s

We separated in 1996, and I starting drinking during the week – something I had always hated about my husband. I told myself this was bad and that I should not be doing this. I had thoughts during the marriage of taking my life, and again after I left, even though I knew I had done the right thing for us all to leave. Then I met the man that was to take me to the gates of hell with him!

My now ex-husband was living near us, so he would take the girls at the weekends and this allowed me to go out more.

1997

We had a serious car accident, and I came off worst – my right leg was shattered at the femur and I had a fractured skull. My ex-husband brought my youngest daughter to visit me in this state in the hospital, and I screamed at him to get out. But he was drunk and just kept laughing at me.

Laid up for weeks in hospital, my obsession with my new man kicked in. We had been together for around a year – the one-night stand who stayed. I kept wondering where he was and what he was up to while I was lying in hospital. We declared deep love for each other, yet really it was more of a lustful relationship.

From then until 2001-2, I deteriorated into an aggressive, hostile, angry woman, blaming everyone else for my problems. And, boy, did I have problems. But I was unable to realise that I had created them. People would be well meaning in telling me what to do, but I liked it when someone told me HOW to do something.

My family threatened to have Social Services come and take my children away, and I told them in no uncertain terms where to go and to mind their own business. I dabbled with speed bombs and was violently ill with the come-down from them, then I tried cannabis, as the painkillers I had made me violently sick. The cannabis killed the pain and numbed my head from the reality of my circumstances.

My youngest sister had come to help after the accident, as I couldn't even bend down to take washing out of the machine. As she and her then partner were also taking cannabis, we all abused drugs together. We would take bongs and what was called buckets, but my body reacted violently to some of these activities and, luckily, I stopped. But not with alcohol. I would swear off drink and be ill for a whole day and then mentally low for another two, but then I'd pick up and do it all over again. Looking back, I was drinking alcoholically then.

Some of the people coming into my home at that time were not a healthy bunch. I ended up keeping drugs in the house for the local dealer. One night he came in looking for payment from my relative and held a knife to his throat. But I thought this was 'normal' for the life I was now leading. It was certainly a far cry from the wee lassie from the village running free!

I accepted my sorry lot, but had an inkling somewhere that this was not healthy. I just could not seem to stop the train of insanity getting faster and faster!

My three daughters were subjected to mental, physical, and emotional abuse... BY ME! Their mother. They would have to hang around pubs, and I would throw money at them to 'Go to McDonald's, will you?' while I would be out drinking.

I'd become a drunk!

I blamed the man I was living with. I blamed my mam and dad. I blamed the world!

I had to return to hospital for five separate operations on my leg, was on anti-depressants, and was seeing a counsellor for PTSD from the accident.

But I tried so many different ways to try to change our situation. I would not go out with my partner, or I would go out but just drink coke. I would follow wherever he went, to try to pacify him so that he would not get violent.

If I drank, too, the violence was worse; I'd waken to blood-stained walls and bedsheets, or holes in doors and walls, with absolutely no idea of what had occurred the night before.

Every time my partner went to find work away from our town – mainly in London – I would decorate the house, singing, 'I'm going to paint that man right out of my hair!' But I didn't.

One morning as I came into the bedroom, my partner's foot was sticking out of the bed and I instantly sunk my teeth into his big toe! He leapt out of the bed and punched me on either side of my face, making my two eyes swell black and blue within minutes. He was shouting, 'Look what you made me do!' and I was yelling, 'Look what you did to me!'

I became a self-harmer in my 30s, hacking at my leg with a knife. I became a drink and drug abuser. One night I reversed the car down the street to escape from a violent outburst, and when I returned there were knives above every door in the home and my partner was gone. The police had come and taken him away, and I could not sleep as I feared him coming back.

As I said earlier, when I finally arrived in Al Anon, I believed the people there were crazy and I was furious that they should suggest my life was unmanageable. As far as I was concerned, I was managing just fine and keeping everyone ok, thank you very much. The truth is, they never suggested that; it was the way I took it. At that stage in my life, I took everything personally and I made assumptions about everyone else. I had no idea that I was actually mentally ill.

When I finally had to look at my part in my life, it was not pleasant to experience the guilt and shame at how the violence towards me stopped from the day I entered the doors of these meetings. What did that say about me? I had to own up that I was controlling, manipulative, aggressive, an abuser! Was there any good in me at all?

Another level of victimhood ensued along with low grade depression, though I had learned how to hide that.

The violence towards me stopped but the verbal abuse and aggression prevailed, yet I was shown how I contributed to the violent part. Of course, I still tolerated completely unacceptable behaviour from others, and I went into a different kind of victimhood as I made my way around my whole family, apologising for bringing shame to them all. I wanted to make amends, and our relationships improved at that time.

But I would go to festivals and parties, and become the weekend drinker once again. It was a culture thing. At the meeting it was suggested we support and encourage our alcoholic loved ones and friends, yet I wanted to prove I wasn't alcoholic, even though I was drinking at these events. I was consuming copious amounts, but now it was usually only the one night! And I would be so ill next day.

I hadn't known about any processes to deal with grief, but through the study of counselling and psychology at college, I finally realised I had never been taught how to deal with my emotions around death. I hadn't been taught how to communicate my emotions in a responsible manner. 'Stop that crying, don't be so sensitive, stupid girl, etc. etc.' – those are the messages I'd taken on board all my life, and those messages had stuck within my body as beliefs. Now, these words to a highly functioning sensitive person stick hard. They maybe don't to another who can throw them off easily. But I didn't.

Finally, things were improving and life was getting better for me. Even my daughters appeared to be happier. My youngest daughter and I attended college together at the time after her sisters had left home, and our relationship improved for a while.

I was quite happy being on my own, because I felt I knew the type of man I would like to be with. Cosmic ordering was all the rage then, so I wrote out my ideal man, but I knew it didn't matter if I ever met anyone as I was happy alone. I had some more mystical experiences where I would feel I was at one with 'God', though I didn't tell anyone as I didn't expect them to understand. I was in love with God and didn't need another man in my life (I still felt God to be a man, though I didn't notice that until later).

I also decided at this point that I would take the time to really go through the steps and trust that there was a Divine plan, and if it meant taking me longer than one a month then so be it! I was at the mercy of this Higher Power I was now choosing to call God!

Chapter Eight
May 2008

'Being on a spiritual path does not prevent you from facing times of darkness… it teaches you how to use the darkness as a tool to grow.'

Katie Mottram, *who wrote 'Mending the Gap'*

STEP 5: 'Admitted to God, to ourselves, and another human being, the exact nature of our wrongs.'

This month I attended two conventions which went with Steps 4 and 5, which I was doing at that time. One meeting was in Dundee – the annual Scottish – where the theme was 'A New Beginning'.

The second was in Thurso (Step 5) which was near my home soil, so I stayed with my mam and dragged her along to the convention. The theme there was 'Freedom to Choose'.

By that stage, I had experienced guilt, humiliation, and anger, where I learned to name my feelings, yet now we were going in deeper! Now, I went into shame, and the darkness came. I had to realise how I had come to this point in my life, but I struggled with this step because the past was now being revealed to me, and all my shortcomings reared their ugly heads. However, I also felt blessed to have the people in my life who had walked this walk before me and who loved me as I was. They did not have any judgments on the hurt and harm I had caused my children, my family, and others. If they did have judgments, I was oblivious to them... probably because I was shrouded in the shame of it all. I wore that shame daily inside me, while smiling on the outside.

We talk about spectrums in life, and I was on the spectrum of shame. The warm, cosy blanket of denial was being pulled from me.

With the help of Angie, Rosemary, and many others, I had mustered the courage to end the so-called relationship with my partner. I believe I said it with love in my heart, because I realised that I felt compassion and detachment with love for someone who was clearly unwell mentally, emotionally, and spiritually. I needed to recognise this in myself first, though. It is said that sometimes the person who is affected by another's drinking and other substance abuse sprees can be sicker than the drinker. I have witnessed this many times. I also understand it is so much easier to keep a blanket of denial wrapped tightly around us because the shame and hurt is too much to bear.

Eventually, I ended the relationship on the phone, and he knew – as I did – that it was finally over. Most of our interactions had been by phone for some time, because I would not allow him to come to my home when he was drinking. Physically, our relationship had been pretty much over for a couple of years, yet I had struggled to let go emotionally; the mental threads were still attached.

When I started college that year, I occasionally ran into him and I'd react towards some other poor soul! Thank God I had the awareness of this programme, which helped me to recognise how I had been triggered by meeting him, so I could make my sincere apologies to whoever happened to be in the firing line. A great book that helped me here was 'Triggers: Creating behaviours that last' by Marshall Goldsmith and Mark Reiter.

I kept working with these books and steps, phoning mainly Angie now, and occasionally a few others. As I got to know people, I would instinctively recognise who could help me or listen to me on whichever topic I was struggling with. I asked Angie to be my sponsor for this step and the rest, while Rosemary was helping me with meditation.

As part of the teaching of this step, the message I was being given was that I should 'put on my own oxygen mask first'. When travelling on an aeroplane, most of us have heard the cabin staff detail emergency procedure and advise adults to put on their own oxygen mask first before helping a child to put on theirs. My initial argument to this was, 'Yes, but... what about your child?' The counter-argument to that was: 'But what if you see to your child first, and you die? Who will be around to look after your child?'

Putting my own needs first was a completely new concept for me. Even though I was riddled with selfishness and deceit, any loathing was aimed at myself as the veils were being lifted for me to see the damage of the train wreck I'd left and how I'd contributed to that damage. It is not pleasant to start to see yourself in such situations, but I was beginning to recognise the consequences of the choices I'd made over the years.

I suppose confession within religion is usually associated with Catholicism, but it is a ritual within many cultures. This step certainly helped me to know that I was perfect in my imperfections. As part of the step, this type of confession is to be held with someone whom you trust implicitly and who you know will not judge you, simply because they will have complete understanding.

I picked Angie as the 'other human being' to confess my character defects to, because I felt safe with her. I felt she had more experience within the programme and had gone through the steps herself. She loved me, didn't judge me, and was full of compassion for my defects because she had many similar ones. We mirrored each other's inadequacies and fear which had brought us to this point.

With the worksheet of assets and defects, I found I had more assets ticked off than defects. Angie suggested I should think back to when I had first fallen through the doors of Al Anon, and consider how I would have ticked the boxes then. This made perfect sense to me, and showed me how far I had actually come.

My strange experience on the sofa had opened me up to new ways of looking at life.

I realised that I could reach forgiveness for myself and others if I just kept moving forward. I also realised that I had this pattern of relying on others to make my decisions for me. I think Angie picked up on this, as she tried to encourage me to make my own decisions without phoning her first. It made me realise that what I had been doing for so long was seeking approval. Approval from my parents especially. My inner child was screaming for this attention, and really from me; no-one else.

I have heard that there is only one true addiction – to love. We crave love, so seek it through alcohol, substances, food, sex, shopping, gambling, and in many more ways. We seek it from the moment we exit our mothers' wombs, depending on the type of birth we experienced. Depending on our womb experience even.

I had been led to psychology through attending college, and although I had known that Dr Carl Jung had played a part in the Steps Programme, I became more interested in his work. I particularly loved to look at my dreams and try to figure out what they were telling me.

I heard in the meetings how we were like an onion, peeling off our layers; and Carl Jung also talked about that. He believed we are guided by archetypes, which are energy fields living within us and which have positive and negative sides – as though we have an inner magnet which will attract us towards whatever we need to recognise for healing.

He also said, 'There is no coming to consciousness without pain. People will do anything, no matter how absurd, in order to avoid facing their own souls. One does not become enlightened by imagining figures of light, but by making the darkness conscious.' So here I was, heading into my own darkness.

Any issues we have as adults will attract others towards us as we need to heal. Normally, our parents and family are our first port of call and we learn from them and our educators, but unfortunately this means we are programmed into patterns with our limited thinking mind. We are led to believe that these older people know what is right for us, and we have no idea of the vastness of our unconsciousness and how our dream state talks to us from this place.

Back to my step journey. Step 5 is where vulnerability becomes a strength, whereas I had always perceived it as a weakness. 'Don't wash your dirty laundry in public' was the message which had always run through me, urging me to keep things quiet and to myself. But this message was now releasing itself from my cells. The emotional prison I had closed myself (my-cell) into was opening slowly but surely to an inner dimension I had forgotten. And I held the keys to unlock what lay beneath.

Chapter Nine
June 2008

'Good things happen in your life when you surround yourself with positive people.'
Roy Bennett

STEP 6: 'We're entirely ready to have God remove these defects of character.'

Over the years of going to meetings, the fog had slowly lifted from my muddled mind and I could clearly see that my mental state had become quite distorted. I learned a lot about this through Steps 4 and 5, but there were many more layers still to peel off.

I began to study my family of origin. I immersed myself in spiritual books, soaking the information up like a sponge, and felt ready to change the patterns I had been programmed with from birth which had led me to make so many poor decisions. I was still taking alcohol and smoking, which went hand-in-hand at that time, but I justified that I got enjoyment from both.

Coke and crisps, tea and toast went hand-in-hand, too! I had identified defects and, again, I needed to become willing to let them go; to have my HP remove them. Of course, they wouldn't vanish completely, and I would have to keep working these steps over and over, but I really felt as though I was being given a second chance.

My life was changing; it was happening. There must be a God! It was agony but also ecstasy going through these steps as I came to terms with who I had been and who I was becoming! Yet there was still such a long way to go.

I really wanted to understand as much as I could about this 'Family Disease of Alcoholism' and where I fitted into it. My family did not have alcoholism in it. Did it? The words in the song Amazing Grace 'was blind but now I see' took on another meaning, as I kept moving forward four steps then I would take two backwards.

It felt true to me that Step 4 was the toughest. It meant we were examining our own lives, not another's. And looking within oneself is the hardest journey I have found to date, but the author Scott Peck believes that an unexamined life is no life.

I came across a book that someone had given me many years before but I'd dismissed because I couldn't understand it. I took a second chance to read it –The Celestine Prophecy by James Redfield – and this time, I couldn't put it down.

I believe it has played a big part in many folks having their own spiritual awakening, and I was so enthusiastic that I bought ten copies for friends and family who I thought would read it! I had no idea that some of them would not get it, in the same way that I hadn't in the past! But I just wanted my loved ones to get what I had! I did not think I was preaching, but in hindsight, I probably was. I was so in love with this programme that I believed everyone SHOULD be working with these steps in their lives. The principles they embody are awesome! I even thought of how I could get them incorporated into school curriculums!

It was brilliant to share with Angie the passion and excitement of this programme and what we were learning together. I was like an excited wee child learning all this new 'stuff' about life, and I desperately wanted to go to Peru, which was mentioned in The Celestine Prophecy, even though I never believed such a trip was likely. (In fact, I did get to Peru some years later!)

I was soon noticing that when I owned my part and took responsibility for it, good happenings occurred around me. I started to see the opportunity in the challenges!

I learned about The Secret by Rhonda Byrnes and The Law of Attraction with Esther and Gerry Hicks, often reading five books at a time and trying to incorporate ALL of what I was learning into my life! Conversations with God by Neale Donald Walsh, along with The New Revelations, helped me improve my relationship with God, as I began to understand 'Him'.

My home, which had been hell for so long, was becoming my wee heaven, and I re-mortgaged and did the place up. My sitting room was the last place to be improved. Violent outbursts had happened so often there in the past, but as I intended to be spending most of my time in that room, I wanted it to be special.

I had seen an advertisement for a three-piece suite several months before but hadn't been able to afford it. Some six months later, I was sitting on it! How did that happen? I learned to trust more in my own HP – God! I was by then earning enough money to pay the suite up over a few years, and had found it in the bargain basement, down in price from when I had originally seen the advert. So, my relationship with God was becoming stronger and happier.

Chapter Ten
July 2008

'Freedom is the oxygen of the Soul.'
Moshe Dayan

STEP 7: 'We humbly asked Him to remove our shortcomings.'

The 4th, 5th, 6th and this 7th Step had me attending two conventions this month. I mention the 4th and 5th here, because I went to Angie's to take these steps, which actually led into the 6th and 7th. The first convention was in Helensburgh, near Loch Lomond, with the theme 'A Vision for You' (6th). The second, in Birmingham, had the theme 'LOVE' (7th). I was meeting Angie at Loch Lomond and then heading home with her as my trusted friend (other 'human being'), to lay out my wrongs!

It was a fabulous week, as the sun was shining and we spent the days outside in her garden discussing life, then at night we would attend meetings. All the while we were both smoking cigarettes, along with joints laden with weed. We even went through to Edinburgh to buy some one day! Still in Denial! The difference here was that my life was so much more manageable. But I feel on writing this that these behaviours were NOT good for my body.

Some meetings were run with a top table and opened up to the body of the meeting. Others saw the room share particular topics or discussions, and the chairperson would lead the theme with the agreement of the rest of the group.

I had just informed Angie that I was entirely ready for my next step when my phone rang – it was a meeting in Glasgow, asking if I would do their top table next day on Step 7!

What was humility? What was it to be humble? I was glad I had been forced to re-create myself. Previously, I had been a bunch of mixed-up labels, including daughter, sister, brat, wild child, rule-breaker, dreamer...

Now, though, it was time to become a better human being. To be nicer to myself with my self-talk, and hence nicer to others. It was certainly easier to be nicer to others. In meetings, just putting the kettle on, arranging the cups, washing dishes, or setting out the seats was seen as being in service to others. This step was preparing me for more service to others.

I took on 'jobs' as secretary and treasurer at group and area level. These tasks were rotated every three years, so there was always someone with previous experience who could help me. It meant everyone was given their chance, which I believe is a beautiful way to lead. Not to govern. Don't you feel our country and nations would benefit from these principles? I do.

Each of these steps is powerful in its own right, and this one is no different. It is powerful to become humble enough to see that in the grand scheme of things my mind keeps me limited in its thinking. Yet if I believe in a power greater than me, and I am a part of that, then there is a paradox of sorts that I am both! Finite and Infinite!

I carried on with meditation to calm the crazy thoughts that would storm through this head of mine. One of them was the reference to the WE in the steps. I started to grow a Spiritual ego and would often feel myself judging others when they were sharing; my ego wanted to be superior and a know-it-all. Typing this makes me laugh now, but I cringed with embarrassment when I discovered this about myself. Thank God I had someone to bounce these revelations off and reason things out with. Judging was a big defect I wanted removed. Today, I am much better at recognising this.

A beautiful piece of writing from the spiritual teacher Ram Dass has helped, too:

'When you go out into the woods and look at the trees, you see all these different trees. And some of them are bent and some of them are straight and some of them are evergreens and some of them are whatever. And you look at the tree and you allow it. You see why it is the way it is. You sort of understand that it didn't get enough light, and so it turned that way. And you don't get all emotional about it. You just allow it. You appreciate the tree. The minute you get near humans you lose all that. And you are constantly saying, "You're too this" or "I'm too this" and that judging mind comes in. And so I practice turning people into trees. Which means appreciating them just the way they are.'

That's easier said than done, because we are humans and, as a collective, we are connected to each other, so these defects are pretty much in YOU, too. We learn from each other, and point and stare and judge and obsess. One of the daily reads talks about leaving a suitcase of judgements at the door of the Al Anon meeting and picking it up on the way out. But I believe judging goes on in the meetings, too. In-fact, I know it does. Why? Because I did it! We can see it is a human collective addiction.

Steps 4, 5, 6, and 7 were all covered, and I was still in the month of July. God was on my side! I remember feeling there must be a divine plan at that point, and I cried with gratitude. The literature would tell us that a change of attitude aids recovery. For me, that change was to recognise everything that I was grateful for. That was my starting point, and it led me to my utter self-centredness. Even today, as I write this, I see that I had to deal with many more layers of this defect, because it had been engrained in my psyche for so long.

I was so grateful for Angie and for the 12 Step Programme, and I felt ecstatic. But I was still impatient. As I could really see this programme working in my life when I adhered to the principles of it, I desperately wanted to rush it through at times. I arranged to meet up with my first sponsor, who had stopped coming to meetings for some reason. She told me, 'My wish for you was that you slow down, and it fills me with joy to know you have done just that.'

I had never realised I was so 'busy' or 'fast', but I then realised that she was right. I had been a 200-mile per hour person. If I trusted in this Higher Power, I would have to learn to allow and to have patience. 'God grant me patience… and hurry up about it, please!'

I believe that my heart opened at Step 3 when I had my out-of-body experience. And that experience still makes me smile. To be able to write and talk about it now is so easy, yet back then I was terrified to tell anyone in case they thought I was crazy.

Life was not all plain sailing at that point, though. I was still being tested to remove anger, reaction, and judgment. On one occasion, my sister was driving up the other side of the street waving furiously at me, and I thought, Oh no, I am not in the mood for her today. But she spun her car around and parked behind me as I was going into my house.

She came racing out of her car, complaining loudly about somebody else and what they had done to her. As she followed me in, I turned around and shouted at her to stop. I told her I was heading to work and might be late, so I didn't have time to listen. She said something else which felt like an attack towards me, and I immediately screamed at her that she was a junkie and to get away from me.

This confrontation left me shaking on the inside and out, and I felt awful. By the time I got to work, I was busy texting my sincere apologies for being such a bitch, desiring this would make amends.

But a lesson (gift) was learned that day. You see, nothing had been done TO me. It was my defects of anger and reaction and judgment that had come out to play! What a bitch, I admitted to myself. But I had to own that bitch that day. I had to own her and recognise her and vow to feel her rising before I was nasty to someone again like that. Who best to be your teacher than a family member, though? I had to love my sister for being my teacher that day, even though I felt I was a bad student. I was a good student for making the amends in the best way I could, though, and vowing to do better next time.

The book which helped me here was Debbie Ford's The Dark Side of the Light Chasers. It helped me to name my defects and to explore how I hid, denied, and tried to reject any of my dark sideshows.

It's amazing how these books would show up just when needed, or after an event such as the one with my sister. And I believe it is another example of God at work in my life. Through other people. Of course, these books cannot change our lives. We have to put action in and repeat it until the new is absorbed.

Visualising these defects was something that worked for me, and I gave them names like Angry Annie, or Reactive Ruby, and Judging Jenny. These are archetypes within all of us, but we just don't want to show them to the world. We deny they are there and prefer to show the nicer side of them.

This was the month when my youngest daughter sent me a text message which I saved and wrote down, as it made me cry with gratitude:

Hey, was just having a think. I just want to thank you for moving on with your life and meeting Angie to help you to. You have changed so much and you have brought light to the house now! The new you has made us a lot happier. Even the dog! Thanks, Mum. Keep your head up. Keep smiling. You're doing a great job and I'm glad you're so much happier! Glad you found Al Anon! Luv.

Even now, that message makes my heart smile. We went on to grow together in our own ways, but fell out again and didn't speak for a while; we have a very pendulum swing-type of relationship. But such is life, is it not? It spirals and swings, especially between mums and daughters.

CHAPTER ELEVEN
August 2008

'Forgiveness says you are given another chance to make a new beginning.'
Desmond Tutu

STEP 8: 'Made a list of all persons we have harmed and became willing to make amends to them all.'

God as I had 'known Him' had been sacked and I had hired a new one through accepting my powerlessness (Step 1) by coming to believe (Step 2) that there was another way: thy will be done, not mine (Step 3). I had been given a good starting point for making amends with my inventory (Step 4) while bringing my bitch to the light with some help (Step 5), and if I became ready (Step 6) to have my bitch removed, then humility would step in (Step 7) to show me the way.

Step 8 is about forgiveness. Forgiveness is not about forgetting. It's about letting go of the hurt, I was told. And I loved this. When this is accomplished, then the emotional energy attachment is removed. When the energy attachment is removed, I found I do forget.

Throughout my years in Al Anon, I had made lists of people I had harmed. Now, though, I was asked to make a list of them all... and to only become willing. To become willing was the theme throughout this journey, along with acceptance and surrender.

These steps were a process. One which really started the day I practically crawled through the Al Anon doors. At that time, I knew nothing about processing or integrating anything, and I still didn't while I was studying these steps. But I had to live by them while studying them. Walk my talk.

My list of people I'd harmed was an extensive one, and included someone I had become fixated with and quite cruel to while I was at school on the north coast. I asked around but no-one seemed to know what had happened to her. This step does not allow for justification, just pure honesty about my part. So, I added bully to my list of defects! I had at one time threatened her with a physical beating, which makes me feel sick to think about even now. Maybe I haven't fully forgiven myself.

I was asked to write her a letter with my feelings around the situation, then to burn that letter – not send it. Having forgiveness for myself in my heart was what mattered here. To find her and drag her into something she may have tucked away in her memory bank could possibly reap angst for her, so it was not an option to find her. I have heard many horror stories of people seeking out folks they had hurt, and how this could actually cause more harm. This step was simply about forgiveness; asking for it for yourself and for others.

In my morning prayers, I would ask God for the willingness. And I was learning to listen to my body. We are made of energy. Even our thoughts are energy; living breathing energy. If we give that energy focus, it plays out in our external world. As humans, we have what are called mirror neurons; brain cells which code our own

.and others' actions. As we are social beings, these neurons are activated when we see another. Do you feel yourself getting upset watching someone else upset? Do you laugh when you see or hear another laughing? If so, your mirror neurons are firing.

Back to Step 8!

It was said that my own name might be the first on the list of those I'd harmed, but I had tried many times to forgive myself... and failed. I'm not even sure I have succeeded yet, but I certainly try not to repeat old behaviours which I have recognised as shortcomings. Through the amazing Brené Brown's teachings, I have discovered that vulnerability is a great strength, although I did not realise this until much later. She explained guilt and shame to me on a new level. Guilt meant I had done something wrong. Shame was a much deeper place, where there is something wrong with me. I did a bad thing (guilt); I am a bad thing (shame). In the past, I would say, 'Well, if he had just done this, then I would not have behaved that way.' But this step was teaching me to forgive myself without justifying my behaviour.

My third stint back at college was proving to be both heaven and hell for me. My first time had been after school, just to do something, and I hated it even though I made many friends there. The second time was in Edinburgh, through a youth scheme; that was also just to do something. Yet both these courses gave me skills that I still use to this day.

Third time around, I felt I was in a 'school' environment again, having to study English and arithmetic once again. My inner child was beginning to stir, yet I did not know it then. And I even threw a childish tantrum in the maths class and stormed out shouting, 'I don't need to learn this again! I came to learn complementary therapies, not bloody maths!' How embarrassing!

I quickly became aware that I was being tested again, and I could see how my past was playing out in my present through my behaviours! In came Eckhart Tolle and his book, The Power of Now! He talks about the pain body, which resonated with me. It is another book of awakening for many, but I prefer his other book, The New Earth.

I studied counselling skills and psychology at college and continued to work in the care sector, which was something I loved. I went on to work with various people with different 'issues', ranging from dementia to MS, the elderly, and those with mental illness/health, severe learning difficulties, and disabilities. Finishing up working with children in residential care.

The convention of the month was in Aberdeen, with the theme 'Promise of Hope'. I had recognised now that there was always hope, and had become totally reliant on this programme. I swore I would never stop going to meetings, as I was off all medication.

As I was doing things holistically, addressing the whole – my physical, mental, emotional, and spiritual – I had to see how they all worked together in sync. A looked-after and fine-tuned vehicle runs smoothly when you service it, change the oil, and have it MOT'd or serviced regularly. And my body was now telling me the same. It had actually been telling me that all my life but I had not realised it. Until then, if my body went 'wrong', I just went to the doctor for some pill or other. But that did not always work. This programme worked, though – better than anything I'd ever had from a doctor. While doctors do some fantastic work, none had recognised that I was 'suffering' from alcoholism. All I got offered were anti-depressants, sleeping pills, and Valium.

Someone from the AA fellowship told me that a visit to the doctor had allowed him to be off sick, long term, from his job, with a concoction of medical supplies that he just went out and sold to other addicts. Denial lives at many levels. For this particular man, he was in deep denial about his choice of drug. He would sit in AA telling all how long it had been since he stopped using alcohol, yet he was still taking opiates. Denial is deep in society. And until one is ready to hear, they are deaf.

I still knew I would have to stop smoking at this point. Even though I'd made many attempts to quit over the years, I always returned to this addiction. Since learning and practising Reiki, though, I had found that I was becoming repulsed by the smell of smoke, and noticed it sticking to my clothes and in my hair.

I had taken on the job in the care sector believing I'd be there until pension age, then retire and die! Now I was opening up to seeing this was maybe not true for me.

I was no longer blaming anyone; I was 100% responsible for my life. And as my inner children were coming forward for healing, I could imagine others as innocent little children and have compassion for them.

I learned the word discernment. I had heard it previously, but had not known its full meaning. Now, though, I was starting to listen to my body and to know the decisions that were right for me and those that weren't. It started with buying a new car, funnily enough. I could not decide which colour to get – black or white, diesel or petrol. But at least I could see that I had always relied on others to make my choices or to tell me what to do. I suppose it sounds silly, but it was a major hurdle for me. I had been deeply conditioned to listen to others instead of my own innate system! I was starting to see that my intuition was always spot on, yet I had previously disregarded it by listening to others insist that they knew what was right for me.

I had been so co-dependent of others that my body would go into physical pain when having to make a decision. But now that I was doing complementary therapies, I knew every pain and what emotion it was associated with. For example, I'd had this pain in my neck for a few years that would not shift... until I shifted inner resentments to others. I had made them the pain in my neck!

And, of course, we all know the other pain. Yip! Pain in the butt! Literally, for me. While I had been living in a violent home, I'd suffered from severe haemorrhoids and endured many trips to the doctors and hospital, for elastic bands, injections. Nowadays, I only have this problem if I have something to let go of! Metaphysically, it is said that 'your past has become such a part of your identity that you fear letting go of it' (Page 405 of Metaphysical Anatomy by Evette Rose – she has many more suggestions, and I identified with most). All ailments I have ever had I connected with this woman's work, along with Louise L. Hay's You Can Heal Your Life. This had been my first port of call regarding emotions and physical pain.

We are social animals. We need each other, really. When groups of people get together with similar issues, they connect. This programme saved my life. I was, and will always be, extremely grateful for it. I still tell people about it, and I offer to take them to a meeting when I recognise myself in them.

Now the question was how do I – if I am ready to – make amends to the people on my list?

Chapter Twelve
September 2008

'Sorry, with conviction, needs loving action.'
Lorna

STEP 9: 'Made amends to such people wherever possible, except when to do so would injure them or others' step came into play.'

Step 9 took me down to Dumfries to the Blue Bonnets Convention, where I was told 'You're No Longer Alone'.

It was suggested that I write out three columns: who I would definitely not make amends to; who I might be willing to; and who I definitely would. I believe this step would be suitable for anyone, because as we 'grow' in life we realise that peace within is precious. And to have that, forgiveness is a big part of the journey.

I had no names in the first column; maybe one or two in the second; most were in the third column. I wrote a few letters to people, including my ex-partner, and sent them where I felt I could. Then I burned the remaining letters. It is all about the intention.

Over the years I had abused my own body by allowing it to be used for sex while I craved love. This was mostly done, in all honesty, while I was drunk. But I decided I was going to take a vow of celibacy to heal my body and ask for forgiveness. This still has an emotional charge to it, and is the part of healing which I am at present in therapy sessions about. What is sex to you? What is love to you? These are deep questions. When I was exercising these behaviours, I was what spiritual communities would term 'unconscious'. I was participating in life with others who were unconscious, so I would attract people into my life who would mirror my own self-loathing, and hence be orchestrating abusive and destructive behaviours a lot of the time through drink-fuelled decisions that I would then regret.

That mirror eventually shattered into a thousand-plus pieces, and is still returning to its shiny glory! The pieces now being glued back together are attracting far healthier others. Not for the sex act, I hasten to add, but to see how conditioned we as humans are around the topic of sexuality.

In my generation, if you were a man and had sex with many women, you were slapped on the back and congratulated for being a stud! If you were a woman who had sex with many men, you were used by men and shunned by other women, and called a slut by both genders. You'd be talked about in the village or town where you lived, with plenty of sniggering and comments behind sheltered hands.

I was the only person I know of who held a meeting about sex and intimacy in the years I spent at my home group meetings, but it turned out to open the floodgates for some members and to be embarrassing for others. When I attended the July convention in Birmingham, there were open come-and-go meetings and they had a few people hopping in and out of them. The sex and intimacy meeting had queues outside when it was time for it to start, and they had to take extra seating in and even turn people away. This alone told me how important this topic is.

Even the topic around monthly bleeding was taboo in my youth. I recall running home excited to tell Mam about mine starting at the age of 11, yet have no memory of what followed, other than suffering monthly and calling it 'the curse'. Sadly, I passed on the same crazy information to my daughters. But now, how times are changing! I have met women who hold menstruating parties for their daughters, and the importance of this time for the female is now coming forth into society. Women no longer need to be shamed by the natural cyclic workings of their bodies. There are many books written by some amazing women regarding our bodies and how to work with them. I intend to buy some for my granddaughters! It is a pivotal rite of passage for females.

When I explained a lot of what I was doing to Mam and told her I was going to write her a letter to make amends, she said, 'You don't need to do that, Lorna, just keep doing what you're doing.' And I took this on board.

However, I felt that to say 'sorry' was not enough; actions speak louder than words for me. Eventually, I found I was working with kids in residential care, and that gave me the opportunity to make many amends indirectly to my daughters, who were then away from home.

Of course, I tried to make amends to them directly as well, but as they had flown the nest by that stage, I couldn't tell them what to do, but just listen and offer support. One time, however, when the past was being thrown around, I remember telling them: 'Some of your problems may have my name on them. However, the solution now has yours.'

I have recently again had discussions around these past times, and it feels as though there is peace with two of my daughters. I am not sure about one of them, yet I love them all dearly and am here should they embark on some journey which would lead them to their mother wounding. And I shall keep doing the inner work as long as it is needed and until there is no emotional charge left to the old stories. Have a look at the work of Bethany Webster on the mother wound. You can find information on her website at: https://womboflight.com/

The children I was working with at that time allowed me to make amends in my life, and I really loved that job. I was working there through an agency, and it was a bit like being my own boss – I believe I was being ushered gently by my HP to be running my own business in later years.

I was making amends to myself by showing kindness to others, and that in itself caused a ripple effect around me. However, I still had a way to go to cherish and know my worth. I was told it was 'a work in progress', but having relationships improving was a good start.

I firmly believe that as long as my amends are made with the right intentions and for the right reasons, then I am not responsible for how others take them. It can, though, be hard to not allow others to affect me. The human Lorna can make assumptions and take things personally, yet I aim to practise 'The Four Agreements' by Don Miguel Ruiz. I suggest you also read his Fifth Agreement, which he wrote with his son, Don Miguel Ruiz Jnr, who also wrote The Five Levels of Attachment. I fall short... often!

Chapter Thirteen
October 2008

'Every day you re-invent yourself. You're always in motion. But you decide everyday.
Forward or backward.'
James Altucher

STEP 10: 'Continued to take personal inventory and when we were wrong promptly admitted to it.'

The convention for this month was near to home again in Dingwall, with the theme to remind me to 'Keep It Simple'. That was something I'd never managed to do; I had made my life complex at every turn, it would seem. But it was becoming easier now, through the loving guidance of the programme and the people in it.

I was trying not to be so hard on myself, and the joy with this was I always had someone to bounce things off. I could brainstorm with another and reason things out with them. This step would help me to keep maintaining my changes on moving forward.

I was becoming too aware to not be aware, and could recognise quickly when I would fuck up and immediately apologise or do whatever was needed to make amends. I had a daily practice I kept to and would journal in the morning and at night, and keep sweeping and cleaning. This is where the ancient Hawaiian practice of Ho'oponopono came to me. There is lots of literature available on this topic, mainly by the author Joe Vitale and his great book, Zero Limits.

As I said previously, I had found Carl Jung through this programme and then again when studying psychology. He had this to say on journal keeping:

'I should advise you to put it all down as beautifully as you can – in some beautifully bound book, it will seem as if you were making the visions banal – but then you need to do that – then you are freed from the power of them....

Then when these things are in some precious book, you can go to the book and turn over the pages and for you, it will be your church – your cathedral – the silent places of your spirit where you will find renewal. If anyone tells you that it is morbid or neurotic and you listen to them – then you will lose your soul – for in that book is your soul.'

In my case, this book is my Soul!

He was talking here about journalling your dreams at night, but for me writing in a journal is healing in itself. At that time, I would write out my dreams within my daily journal setting, but today I have a separate dream journal. At present, I am also working with an amazing woman who is a Carl Jung Analyst www.faranakmirjalili.net and I am working through the Reclaiming the Mythical Feminine course. This involves writing and drawing out my dreams. These images and symbols are a way of connection with the collective consciousness, and are really deep levels of 'stuff' to be brought up.

Through my daily journalling at that time, I learned to observe my thoughts, and it was very revealing to see what was going on in my head. I can have quite a laugh at what I think about. Are you aware of your thinking mind? Again, Mindfulness helps.

At the age of 45, I sat with another lady who, initially, I was scared of; scared of the power she exuded. She stood firmly with her Higher Power. After a chat at her kitchen table, another layer of my denial was whipped off when she announced, 'So what you're telling me is that you've only just let go of your mammy's apron strings?'

I was horrified and was about to bellow, NOooo, when I suddenly realised she was right! I had been in a co-dependent pot with my mother forever, and would dump all my shit at her door.

Once this mask of denial was removed from me and I saw the truth of my life, I became inwardly depressed. I never let anyone know this, other than trusted close friends, and I certainly never mentioned this to my family. My ego was kicking and screaming due to the changes I was making in my life, because the ego mind wants to keep us in the place it knows best, and awareness opens a door to a multiverse of questions that the ego mind cannot possibly take in. Through this journey, the demons that lie in the shadows have to come forth. I feel this is where religion and a lot of spiritual communities can bypass the shadow work needed to expand awareness.

Demons for me are my defects. They live deep within me and need to be rooted out again and again, in the same way that our gardens have horrible weeds that need to be pulled by the root. Otherwise, weeds have a habit of re-growing. Then there are the wildflowers. They are so stunning, yet I was told as a child to stay away from some because they were poison. Weeds and wildflowers grow within us metaphorically. In my case, I need to tend to the poisonous ones and acknowledge them with love.

Once we feel into our bodies and ask our hearts the truth, people will arrive in our lives who can lead us to our own truths, and harmony can be restored on the planet. We are all connected and interconnected. As with the mirror neurons, the world leaders that we are pissed off with now are actually showing us what is within us that needs to be brought forth to heal. This will piss you off!

I came to all these realisations through the foundations of these Steps and continuing to see their power in my life as I unpeeled the onion of life. Remember, the onion has strong symbolic meanings for us. Tears. More tears. Through my spiritual journey, I have learned that I have incarnated here many times over many lifetimes, and experienced many of the human experiences we may read or hear about throughout history. Okay, I totally get that some folks will say this is crazy talk. That's what we do as humans – we slate others and their belief systems. I have done it myself many times. But it is time for that to stop, and just to accept others as they are and where they are on their journey of consciousness.

I urge you to stop reading for a few minutes, look in the mirror, take some deep breaths, and ask yourself, 'Who am I?' This is particularly important if you are feeling stuck in life or pissed off with any aspect of your life. It's time to take responsibility for your own life and know that when you do so you are also helping everyone else.

As you have probably realised by now, I am a gatherer of information through my own experiences, and if I am invited into another's world to share anything I may have experienced and resonated with, I will gladly do so. I am not here to argue or have complex discussions with anyone; simplicity is my life purpose. It has taken me over five decades to reach this point and it has been worth every step… even though I did not think so at the time. Remember, it is the thought that counts! (That's the title of another great book worth reading, by Dr David Hamilton.)

We all carry out rituals daily, don't we? Some may feel this is to do with religion. Well, I had to become religious about making my Step 10 inventory a daily practice, along with meditation and journalling and praying. Am I religious? No. Do I believe in God? Yes, in the context of believing in an intelligence energy where WE all dwell and IT dwells in US.

There are other rituals I carry out daily: I waken up; I use the toilet; I brush my teeth; I shower; I wash my hair; I eat. These are all rituals I carry out for my human form to stay in a condition that nourishes it. I also now run, walk, cycle, swim, and exercise in ways I love. All these rituals, or activities, keep me alert and aware of life in and around me. For me, it is imperative that I get out and study how nature plays her role, and I can feel how I play my part within that, too. This is Soul 'work'.

Taking daily inventory led me to maintain this type of lifestyle. As a holistic living person, I can then assist others to do the same. I am happy in my chosen 'job'.

I have learned that life is all about perceptions, and this book lays out my reality and truths as I have experienced in this lifetime. If my story has awakened something within you, I am forever grateful. There have been even more changes since writing this book that I may tell someday.

I am someone who does not want to upset or piss people off intentionally. I learned to shout louder as a toddler and carried this into adulthood, which must have been hard to be around for many people. I was, however, also very kind, affectionate, and nice to people, but high energy, exhausting if not monitored, and wore my heart on my sleeve. Throughout my journey with alcohol, I became arrogant and eventually nasty, aggressive, and violent. This is no-one else's fault. It just happens to be my story.

I finally took that window of opportunity to change, and now I have a new way of living that life for the greatest good of all. (Have you noticed that three-quarters of the word good makes God!) I do not need to convert anyone. I just share my experience. If that resonates, great; if it doesn't, that's also great. I ask that you do not judge. Just witness my writings.

Chapter Fourteen
November 2008

'Until you make the unconscious conscious, it will direct your life and you will call it fate.'
Carl Jung

STEP 11: 'Sought through prayer and meditation to improve our conscious contact with God, as we understood Him, praying only for knowledge of His will for us and the power to carry that out.'

As a child born into a 'Christian' family, prayer had always been on my knees or in bed, just before sleep. I recall 'As I lay me down to sleep, I pray the Lord my Soul to keep, if I should die, before I wake, I pray the Lord, my Soul to take, God Bless, Mam and Dad...' and everyone else's name I could think of. We also had assembly in school every morning when the whole school would recite the Lord's Prayer.

I used the Serenity Prayer when my dad was dying. 'God grant me serenity, to accept the things I cannot change, courage to change the things I can, and the wisdom to know the difference'. It was a lifesaver for me then and on many other occasions, as I have already explained.

I had deep religious trauma running through my cells, which became apparent after my stint attending church again. But I had friends who were not self-proclaimed Christians, yet they walked and talked kindness and sincerity towards others without apparent judging. These were, and still are the friends I hang out with. They are authentic in their values of life. If we, as humans, are contagious, then I want to be around upbeat, kind, unjudging people. I was one of the biggest sceptics around, about everything, proclaiming I had an open mind, until my sofa experience.

I had started meditating long before taking this step, and with the help of Rosemary I did, and still do, have great experiences. I sought out different meditations through Tibetan Buddhism and Mindfulness. I delved into Eastern cultures and found lots of new information. I did not recall learning all this in school. Some people learn it when they start travelling physically. I had not done this. I was led to the information through reading and meeting others.

By that stage in my life, I was studying the steps thoroughly, taking what I liked and leaving the rest, but sometimes still could not see how well I was getting and growing. Speaking out loud a lot of the time to God (prayer) and then listening for an answer (meditation) in whatever way that would be, became a daily practice. In the beginning I was praying for everyone else; as I was recognising my own defects of character, I would see them in others, too. 'Spot it, you've got it,' I would hear from others. And I learned to become aware that if anyone pissed me off, it usually meant there was something deep in me which needed attention.

I prayed for my family, my ex's sobriety, and my peace of mind. I would pray for the knowledge of 'His' will for me. Was I following the right path? Signs could come in various ways – through a movie, a book, another person, finding coins, white feathers. Others would say, 'That feather is from a seagull,' or 'Someone dropped that coin.' Maybe so. But to me, it was a sign to remind me that I am loved, to assure me that I am protected. Angie would say, 'There's no mistakes in God's world, hen.'

The world we live in became quite symbolic in its teachings and this was the start of another route to take. The multiverse talks to us constantly. To find the conscious contact, I still had the old belief that 'God' was a male essence. I had stopped believing that 'He' was some bearded man sitting on a cloud above me watching every move I made and would punish accordingly if I was a bad girl. The wonderful woman who helped me see my denial in my relationship with my biological mother would refer to God as She. I never questioned her about that, yet on my own journey it has led me to a feminine essence within me. This masculine essence is also within me. These are within you, too. Part of my journey is to marry these two within me – the Holy Trinity. I have since discovered that there are many parts of me that needed to be reclaimed, and I am willing to be reunited with Her! And Him!

I love to listen to Neal Donald Walsh's cd's as he alternates between a male and female voice as God. So, I refer to either He or She. In the film The Shack God is a black woman. His will showed me to keep doing what I was doing, to be kind and courteous. To me, this is carrying a strong powerful message of Her will; to realise that this HP is also my family's HP and everyone else's, was another revelation with this step. (Did you like how I alternated there from God being a he and a she?)

I believe that there is One Infinite Intelligence and we are like a grain of sand within that energy. There are galaxies, stars, and planets and much more within this intelligence. We are like minute cells on a planet, which is another minute cell within a universe, as another minute cell within galaxies, and WE get to play as humans within it all! What a joy that can be! What an honour to be human in these times!

The planet is made of mainly water, as are we. Women, especially, move with the tides with their monthly menstruation. Everything is interconnected, and when we manage to sit in silence, that divine part of us can filter through the noise with our breath and practice, practice, practice. We go to the gym to tone and exercise muscles, and we lose that tone if we do not keep disciplined in doing what we need to do for change to occur. It's the same with making conscious contact through meditation. This for me is food for my Soul.

All this brought me to the work of the Human Design, and ultimately the Gene Keys by the lovely Richard Rudd. From his teachings, I went deeper into the feminine aspect of a God, and he has a beautiful prayer for the Goddess:

Our Lady, who lives at the heart of all form, Hallowed be thy name. May thy Queendom come, may thy Will be done That heaven may come to earth. Please allow me this day to drink from your sacred, silver spring and forgive me my forgetting as I learn through your Grace to return all non-love with Love. And take me by the hand and lead me step by step into the patient valley of your heart, for yours is the earth, my body and my life for ever and ever, Amen.

I now study these keys and follow the Golden Path. I am also following my inner authority and strategy, which is highlighted through the Human Design. On finding out my type, I can see that my life was run on a not self-theme. I can see that the 12 Steps were my foundation to building up my Spirit through the guidance of my Soul. I now feel that my Spirit aspect is the Masculine (Adam) essence within me, The God; I feel that my Soul is the Feminine (Eve) essence within me, The Goddess. Mother Father God, if you like. They live within me, which is the body (Eden). I pray to both these aspects as the One, and ask for the guidance to flow through me for the Highest Good of all.

When I say of all this, I mean the collective consciousness, so I am praying for YOU, too. I learned this at the base level of 'the wisdom to know the difference'. I had a battle with that part of the Serenity Prayer for some time, until I could fathom out what was my ego mind and what really was my heart. I developed a spiritual ego where I thought I knew what was right for others. I do not. Now, I aim to guide them to themselves. But only if invited to do so.

Each of the Al Anon Steps leads nicely into the next, so I could start to see that and trust in the mystery of life. It was like a conveyor belt pulling me along gently. This was a miracle. I was no longer alone. At times, I might feel lonely, yet I would never have to feel alone again.

The convention I attended was in Fort William (11th) and if I recall 'Keep it Simple' was the AA theme while ours was 'Serenity, the Priceless Gift'. Aaaaahhh, just writing that makes me feel it!

Time for a quick and simple review of how far I had come through the steps.

I had to admit defeat and realise that I was the problem, and that I had created a life of unmanageability. I then accepted that I had become mentally unwell, yet rewiring my mind could make change possible if I tapped into a Source better equipped than me to help – all the while becoming willing. I looked deep into myself and family of origin, and told a trusted friend of how bad my behaviour had become. I relied upon this Source to remove the demons that would keep coming to call, while amending the behaviours I recognised as not helpful to anyone. I had to keep guard at the door of my mind so that thoughts would be caught before any action was taken. I could do this by keeping quiet and listening to my inner space for the love to govern.

I became happy to be with Lorna and to study her! To be alone and not feel lonely. To be alone and not have a TV blaring, or be on the phone, to enjoy my own company through painting or just to sit in silence. I had never been able to do that before; I'd always needed to be doing something. I became addicted to reading books. You know, I think some addictions are good for us. It's just about getting a balance. Running or exercising can become an addiction, and it's said around the 12 Step arena that we swap one addiction for another. I would say my main one is over-thinking.

I am now classed as the Crone, the Wise Woman. I'm not sure about that, but I have certainly gained a complete new inner-standing (understanding) of life, and I believe there is so much more to learn that I could not do in one lifetime. I have dabbled with different belief systems, and generally just take what I like and leave the rest.

One of the concepts of Al Anon is 'Participation is key to harmony'. So, today I choose to participate in my own life and be 100% responsible for only me now.

It was my discipline with Step 11 which led me to the body. Somatic meditation takes me inside myself.

I battled with yoga for some time and could never decide if I needed it in my life. I preferred Pilates, but I hated it every time I went to a class.

Anyway, I then found yoga nidra! Oh wow! I love it. It takes you inside your body. It's an amazing modality. So now I do stretches for my body that I like, and I feel the benefit. I enter within through yoga nidra.

Some people do walking meditation, others do running (Chi). I started running when I was 49 years old and have so far entered three 5ks, seven 10ks, nine half marathons, one marathon, and a triathlon. I enjoy it. It gives me fresh air. I get lots of insights (like the cover for this book) while out running, and I notice how nature is always speaking with us if we wish to have that conversation. Signs and wonders!

So, truth time. I fail at this step on many occasions. I am not consistent. But thanks to discovering Human Design, I see that I do not need to be consistent, and I hear that 'thank you' is the only prayer we need to say. I say it inwardly a lot. It's the meditation part I fail on, because I allow my mind to chatter so much. It takes me a long time to fall into that quiet still lake within me.

I keep trying, though. Sometimes I succeed, other times I don't. That is ok.

Chapter Fifteen
December 2008

*'When we give cheerfully and accept gratefully,
everyone is blessed.'*
Maya Angelou

STEP 12: 'Having had a spiritual awakening as a result
of these steps, we tried to carry this message to others,
and to practise these principles in all our affairs.'

Ok, so the 12 Steps had been studied and applied to the best of my ability at this time in 2008. I had done it! In under the year.

Remember, I had been in this fellowship, hammering meetings and conventions and cups of tea for nearly six years by then. What next? I had changed... to the delight of myself and others. Yet I was still smoking cigarettes and joints, depending on who I was hanging out with. So, I did not yet have mental sobriety, as I believe that smoking is a smokescreen to deeper issues. If it wasn't – and we know the health risks of smoking cigarettes and cannabis – then why would we do it? Yes, I know the health benefits of the cannabis oils now and I wholly agree with them, yet the arena in which I smoked it was not about that.

I was back at college and loving it. I had also made numerous new friends, but would still go to them believing they knew best for me at times. I kept aiming at following my Soul's lead through conscious contact with my Higher Power.

The last convention I attended was actually in the month of November, in Skye (12th). The theme was 'Joy in Service' which coincided with the 12th Step. When I arrived on the Friday, I was asked if I would participate for Al Anon by sharing at the AA's top table public meeting on the Saturday night. Fear crept in about putting myself 'out there', so I asked if I could let them know the next day.

I went for a walk in the beautiful hills of Skye and found solace and serenity there, handing over my concerns and fears to God. Somehow, I had known before I arrived that I was going to be asked to participate. So, how could I go against Her will for me?

That Saturday night, I sat with a crystal in my hand and these steps staring down at me from the top table. It was like a divine plan. I could look at these steps and refer to my year just gone and how Al Anon had worked for me. I talked about my journey with them, how another's drinking had affected me, and my part in that. I talked about how violence had stopped in my home from my very first Al Anon meeting. And although aggression had not left, my courage had increased. Most of all, I talked about how, as a mother, I felt so bad about bringing my daughters up in a really unhealthy violent environment.

There was one more event that year to attend, and that was the Regional Service Seminar (RSS) for Al Anon. Every four years a United Country would host this event, and 2008 was Scotland's turn. It was the icing on the cake for me. We had workshops, lots of fun, and great food and company.

The weekend after the event, I collapsed on my sitting room floor and cried, then cried some more. I felt desolate and bereft! I felt alone again! I felt bloody awful. The majority of my friends that I felt closest to did not live close to me, they were all in the Central belt, and I felt I didn't have anyone to hang out with in Inverness.

My phone started ringing, but I did not answer it. I was back in the 'poor me' mode, but I did not realise this was an immense healing session for me. That only came with hindsight. These were healing tears of release! And after my meltdown passed, I was happy to spend a lot of time on my own.

I realised I had put my dear friend Angie on a pedestal. She had been steeped in the programme for one year longer than me, and because she could attend more meetings than me, I felt that she knew better so I handed my power over to her a lot of the time. We drifted away from each other and I felt sad. I didn't need her any more, and she sent me a nasty text after I had stayed at her home one weekend without participating in smoking and a late night.

She did apologise a couple of years later, but we couldn't rekindle our close friendship. God rest her Soul, as she took cancer and left her human suit. She came to me in a dream a few nights beforehand and I knew she was about to die. We had our farewell in my dream. It was lovely and felt very real to me.

I attended meetings outwith Inverness at that time. One week I went to Elgin on the Monday and Wednesday; I went to Tain on the Tuesday; and I did Inverness on the Thursday and Saturday. I took the Friday night off because I was shattered. I was drained from it all, but I knew the programme had saved my life. I was addicted to the 12 Step Programme! Holy shit!

In January 2009, I stopped smoking cigarettes, but continued to take weed on occasions, even though I knew it would cause hash hangovers or mild panic attacks. I told myself I was not taking it a lot, and only with specific people, but that was me justifying my behaviour again. Thankfully, it was not anything like it had been prior to recovery, though.

It was now six years since I'd asked the alcoholic to leave the home, and he'd been in and out of it until Step 3. For the past few years, I would not and could not tolerate drinking as he did, and was not even partial to it myself by this time, other than a Baileys at Christmas time. Occasionally, I did take one too many again – at a friend's house one night, and in 2010 at a music festival – but I came to realise that I was doing it to fit into a social setting with particular people. The saying 'bad habits, dying hard' comes to mind.

I became involved with an old friend from childhood, and we would smoke weed together when we met up. That came to a halt at a barbeque she had. I knew weeks in advance that it would be the last night I would smoke it, and I was ill from it that night. Since then, I have been able to see the truth of that substance, too, and the denial within it. All these substances alter the mind for me in a way that has caused me distress and mental disorder. Just like alcohol, though. If you smoke or drink, that is ok. All about balance, remember.

As I evolve, I have found that my circle of friends changes. They now tend to be the ones who support and stand by my principles; the rest I reject. My sensitivity or insensitivity towards other people and their specific needs is based on a resonance with my own principles. If I'm evolving towards others' ideas and ideals, I want to either fix them because I feel they may be broken in some way, or I can see their potential if they want to change. I've realised that I have a tendency to hang on, hoping for that to happen, but

I just waste energy within the relationship. Now I know to just leave things alone.

Step 12 tells me to 'carry this message', and I still inform people of Al Anon, where meetings are being held, and offer to take them if they feel too shy or anxious to go alone. But the message I can carry is one of kindness to a suffering human being. Kindness in all our affairs.

The journey through these steps has been enlightening and has led me into my inner space. I had searched and looked for love in my external world through many means, but was only ever happy fleetingly. Now I realised I could be content, and that was okay. I could be an example. Through the work I now do, I can divert people towards recovery if they are asking me for help, but I do not go out looking to save anyone.

I am constantly talking with my-self around the thoughts that pop up, and I am blessed to have my partner and my rock in Robert, whom I met at the Fort William convention in 2010. I was asked to do the top table as an Al Anon participant that weekend, and I met Robert the night before my talk. We clicked and danced and had a fantastic time connecting, but I knew that I had to take this relationship slowly.

Robert had been sober in AA for 15 years when he had a complete breakdown and attempted suicide. He, too, had become addicted to the programme and to helping others.

We spent every day talking on the phone – 40 hours in total the first week. He would challenge my whole being, because he had done the 12 Steps of AA and wanted to know the difference between the two programmes. I found that ours was more compassionate towards the suffering alcoholic, and part of that compassion for me was to let people go from my life when I was feeling dragged down by their behaviour.

We would meet up in Glasgow or Edinburgh when I was down at Angie's, and have lunch and spend a few hours in each other's company. We got on really well, and there was a tangible chemistry between us.

He eventually made it up north to visit me, but slept on the sofa bed. Although we both knew our feelings were pretty intense, I wanted to take that side of the relationship slowly.

Robert told me that he'd had a terrible stutter as a child and had undergone speech therapy, but this stutter returned when he suffered his breakdown. (We like to call these events 'breakthroughs' not 'downs'.) When I first met him, he was in a homeless unit and in recovery again.

Through long discussions about our lives, he admitted that he had thrown himself into his AA programme to the point of neglecting his family, yet he had tried so hard to make amends to them with holidays and periods staying away from alcohol. Unfortunately, he was still away from the home a lot because he was attending so many meetings. Still the absent father, just in a different way now.

He needed to do that to stay sober, but all his deep core issues started to come to the surface. Just as they had done for me. This is what happens when you dive deep into yourself! It's why a lot of people will just stop there and not delve into their defects. Many will keep going to meetings but talk about not really having to work with the steps or not having to look too deeply into the teachings. Both Robert and I agree that this has sadly helped to dilute the message of the 12 Steps, and it can cause people to walk away from them without improving their lives.

To this day, Robert still helps the suffering alcoholic – and I am in awe of this. He has not thrown himself into it the way he had done, but he is in constant service to others. He practises Step 12 to the person on the street.

Robert has noticed, like me, that the meetings are different up here. I believe this is because the Highland culture has this underlying theme running through it about keeping our secrets to ourselves, to not wash our laundry in public, to show others that we are 'normal'. So, we are so steeped in the denial of the dark side of alcohol and drinking that the pain of delving into how it really affects us as families or as an individual is keeping us 'sick'. We take the substance to mask our denial over the deep-seated issues that have usually occurred in childhood. We play it down and make jokes about it, yet many families are really suffering.

We deny that there are any issues. For example, if there's an alcoholic horse thief who stops drinking... he is still a horse thief. Have a look at Gabor Mate's talks on addiction on YouTube, and his book, The Realm of the Hungry Ghost.

That moment on the sofa awakened my spirit to show me that I had been brainwashed from childhood with conditioning and programmes of centuries. For me, it was a beautiful mystical experience. A spiritual awakening? Maybe. Finding the Human Design and the Gene Keys has helped me to further release these idiocies and bring me back to the God head, to recognise when an old programme wants to kick in again.

When writing this book, The Council of Critics frequently ambushed me, making me anxious about the reactions of family and friends to my story. But love won the battle and my Spirit came through to help me be open and honest about my journey with the 12 Steps. I only hope that you can see how these steps can help you, too.

Robert's Story:
A small part of it

*'Children are born innocent. Before they are
domesticated, they live in the moment, love without fear,
and don't even think about the opinions of others.'*
Miguel Angel Ruiz

Robert was also born in the swinging 60s; his mother was neurotic, his father a raging alcoholic who at times was violent. He and his older siblings – twins – were born into a mining community, which I suppose these days would be called working class. Their small village had a greyhound track, and through time he became involved with the greyhound community, as both his father and grandfather had before him.

As a child, Robert's life was plagued by uncertainty, due to his alcoholic father's behaviours and his mother's reactions to them. As a result, he became extremely fearful as a small child, developed a stammer, and would wet himself on the occasions when his father came home and was violent towards Robert's mother and older siblings. He was never violent towards Robert.

On one occasion, he remembers his mother stabbing his father in the leg one dinner time, and Robert and his siblings carried on eating their food as though this was normal, the blood spurting from his dad's leg.

There was a family of nine who lived opposite him, in a two-bedroomed house. One of the sons was Robert's childhood friend, so he belonged in their home more than in his own. This family had little food or money, but they made him feel loved and safe. And although there was an alcohol problem there, it did not seem to be as severe as in Robert's own home.

He had a strong relationship with his granny – his saving grace – who Robert believes knew what was happening in his home. But he feels that his mother was jealous of their relationship and also blamed Robert for keeping her in a marriage that was clearly violent.

As a result, he and his mother never developed a loving relationship, even though it is what he craved. And he became an extreme people-pleaser as a result. With his own experience of seeing the extremes of behaviour people will endure and live in because they see no way out, Robert is understanding of others going through similar journeys. And he forgives easily. However, if you hurt him badly, he will not resume any friendship with you.

At the age of 12, Robert's father introduced him to greyhound racing. His father was a known expert with the dogs, and up to all the tricks of the trade. The young boy quickly learned how to gamble and make money through ill-gotten gains, and was introduced to gangsters and go-go girls. This set him on a life of drinking, gambling, and women, as a likeable and popular 'cheeky chappy' not paying attention or achieving anything at school.

I was lucky to have a friend that worked at the BBC in Inverness, who managed to find a TV programme in the 80s which featured Robert's dad. We got a DVD made and I surprised Robert with it. Watching and remembering those times allowed him to release painful memories he had held for years.

When he left school, Robert served an apprenticeship as a wood machinist, yet drink was always his first port of call. Then he met a woman a couple of years older than him, and she fell pregnant. They married and had another daughter a few years later, and by the age of 29 he was – in his own words – a raging lunatic with alcohol, often lying in his own urine and faeces, and believing he was a great guy.

Robert never had a bad word to say about his ex-wife when I met him, only admiration for how she raised their children and did not join him in his drinking sprees. But he kept his drinking away from the family by disappearing from the home for spells – ranging from 2-3 days in the week, to weeks at a time.

Eventually, in a 24-hour period Robert finally stopped drinking and, at the time of writing, has not touched any alcohol for a quarter of a century. How could this be, when he could not stop before, even for his family?

Robert believes, 'No human power could stop me drinking, not even myself; it had to be Divine intervention.' A power greater than himself.

When he and I first met, we realised that we used to drink in the same pub and attend the same club many years before, but had never crossed paths. Obviously, we were never meant to meet up at that time in our lives, as we both had a lot of research and work to do with alcohol in the 80s.

With his experience of working with AA over the years, Robert tells me that more people die in 12 Step Programmes than actually recover. In some circumstances, they can walk away and get worse. And I have seen this happen myself, whether it be with alcohol or other substances or practices.

Basically, where any organisation has its roots with humans, there will be conflict. They are human beings with defects of character, screaming in some instances, and plenty of blame, judgement, and the old finger-pointing going on.

The Truth About Denial

'You cannot live a brave life without disappointing someone.'

Oprah Winfrey

We gather information throughout our lives with our minds (thoughts), and these can grow and grow and flourish until they are firmly embedded. These are our belief systems. They then guide us in our development in the four aspects in which we live: our physical, mental, emotional, and spiritual aspects or bodies, as they are known. These four aspects are intricately woven with subtler bodies that cannot be seen with our physical eyes!

We can believe we are happy and enjoying life OR we can keep these beliefs in the darkness until our lives become so unmanageable there is nothing left but to root out those monsters that have grown in our minds. Some call them demons. Again, it is about perceptions and perspectives.

Perception is how we view a particular situation through our five senses and the personal filters we each have.

Perspective means a way to look at a point of view, perhaps with a particular frame of mind.

They both mean more or less the same thing.

This is why I know that my story – and I suspect Robert's also – will be viewed very differently by others who decide what is a truth and what is not.

I'm someone who wants to avoid confrontation in all ways, yet I find I am better with it now. By writing about and sharing my journey and the research I have conducted, I hope it can help other people to look more deeply at their own situation and how to tackle any problems they may have.

We could all try to get along with each other in whichever small part of the world we live, and make the difference there. Then it can have a knock-on effect and ripple out to others. Let's change the world a mind at a time! A thought at a time!

Take one of your beliefs that can cause you anxiety or distress. Really sit with it, with a willingness to change. Then write about it. There are many ways and many resources out there to dabble in to find your own way. I have shared how I did it, alongside the 12 Step Programme. Both Robert and I had reached our personal rock bottom and by the grace of God were led to sit in meetings with others who had also had enough and embarked on the journey of inner peace.

These meetings saved both our lives, and we developed a new foundation on which to build a new set of beliefs, a new language to talk, and a new way to live our lives. A new toolbox. It is said that an unexamined life is no life – having examined our own lives, that is something we can both agree on.

You have no doubt heard the phrase 'Ignorance is bliss', and many people will remain in that state, declaring that they are right and everyone else is wrong. But it also brings to mind another phrase I read: 'Do you want to be right, or do you want to be happy?'

Both of us felt for many years that we were right and others wrong; we knew best about things. How arrogant the mind can become through the programming and conditioning of our childhoods. And that's not me laying blame. We had both felt 'stuck' and unhappy on the inside, while putting on the human masks to tell the world we were happy. We changed and corrected our minds. Rewired the brain waves.

When we first met, we spent hours on the phone discussing life, our stories, and how we had got to where we were at that point. Robert and I were so excited to be talking with each other about circumstances we felt the same way about, our previous relationships, the parts we played within them, and owning the shit we had caused. We talked about what we had learned and how grateful we now were that others had come into our lives for us to grow and evolve into the humans we were.

We realised that no-one had ever done anything TO us, but FOR us! And that was an amazing revelation! When in victimhood, we believed that the hurts were done to us. But with a new framework and a new set of glasses, so to speak, we could see the blessings from previous relationships, and send love to others who had been in our lives and family members who still were.

It felt so freeing to us both to recognise and honour each other and our individual journeys. It's not what happens to us, it's how we respond to what happens to us. And to see that it is FOR us. It is a process and can take years. So many quick fixes out there. To really examine a life is no quick fix.

When Robert moved in, the first year showed us that we still had excess 'baggage' where relationships were concerned. This tested us and showed us we had to grow together or grow apart. We had regular DMC's (deep and meaningful conversations) and became good at expressing our needs with each other. We hadn't had the appropriate tools to help us in the past, but now we did. And we would pick up new ones, and share and test them together. For both of us, these were new levels of being with another.

The love grew between us without obsessions, pulling, shoving, or judging the other – something I'd never experienced before. Of course, there were arguments, but there was no stomach-crunching fear there for me. We could communicate and express ourselves then fall into harmony again relatively quickly. We can recognise when our inner children are at play, and sometimes space is needed for us to work things out on an individual stage.

As I delved deeper and deeper into my heart and inner worlds, Robert followed, and we trained in Shamanic practices and worked (work) together in this field, thriving and evolving and finding new projects to do, continually expanding our hearts as we move forward through life.

This is still a work in progress for us both. We did go into business together for a while, but that tested our relationship at a deeper level and brought up more issues we had not foreseen. Money became a symbol in our lives, which I believe showed that we both still had low self-worth. All the words that are used around money came to me through the awareness I was gaining through entering into an inner world I had only talked about before.

However, this conjured up even more denial on my part and showed me how I had grown a Spiritual ego along the way, using Spiritual by-passing. That term basically means I was delving into anything with a Spiritual essence and talking about it to others, but avoiding going into the deeper crevices of my own self to dig out even more beliefs that stemmed from my ancestors!

This led me to look into the origins of ancestry and how it travels down the lineage of families. Now I had known this to a certain degree while doing my 4th Step in the Al Anon groups. But this ran deeper, and I started to meet people I could identify with in other ways, who were not my biological family. I could see that some in my immediate family were still affected by the family dis-ease of addictions, and heard from certain members what they all felt about me. My human mind would go into overdrive, and when I voiced truths as I saw them, I would be shot down as a liar.

Despite this hurt, I kept going back to basic slogans I'd learned, prayers I'd said that would keep me engaging in life, and hanging out with people who understood me. Robert maintains he'd never met anyone who would dig deep into their psyche the way I did. But with my experience of the 12 Step Programme, I knew it was vital for my health and wellbeing to keep being responsible and accountable without pointing at others and judging.

Fear was still lingering in the background for me, and I believe it stemmed from the fear of confrontation and physical punishment from adults when I was a child. I often hear adults say, 'I got belted and it never affected me.' Really? I am happy if this is the case for people, I really am. Though…

I would beg to differ. I have met people who, when they go deep into their past, discover that the physical pain they are in today as adults came from childhood thrashings or beltings they received. They would tense up and hold their breaths, causing the physical pain to become locked into their cells, and this would return in later life when triggered by circumstances which revived the memory of those punishments. These could be triggered unconsciously, yet brought to the conscious through physical pain, eg. sciatica, back pain (very common).

As my and Robert's relationship evolved, my family's deep resentments began coming to the surface, and although I could sense and see this, unfortunately they could not. These resentments would manifest in outbursts of accusations towards Robert, and when I tried to talk to them about issues, the response was, 'Typical Lorna, all about her.' From my perspective, I was trying to share an experience around an issue. Was that making it all about me? To them, in their denial, absolutely.

I am ok with all of this today, though I admit it has been tough at times because my family do not really know me. They only remember who I was, so how can they know me now? We don't spend much time together now, and that includes friends from the past. I have discovered that I am not someone who holds onto friends even though I would try so hard to do so. I have realised that I had lessons to learn from all of them before moving onto the next chapter of my life.

We cannot change our past, but we can change how we think about it, so I have changed to knowing these were all experiences I had chosen to have. Every day is a day to co-create and aim to be a better version of ourselves than we were. This throws up many challenges as we 'peel the layers of the onion' by delving deep into our hearts to open them up to love. Hearts that have been broken, hearts that feel like they will not survive the stress of human life. Yet we survive. And today, I thrive.

It's a human trait to put masks on and aim to be nice, and not allow others to see a side of us even we do not like. Hell, we might not even know that side either, because we have been busy distracting ourselves with other things. To quote Lao Tzu (a Chinese philosopher and the accepted author of the Tao Te Ching – the main text of Taoist thought): 'If you can correct your mind, the rest of your life will fall into place.' And this has certainly been our experience.

Most people make stories up about others as they see fit. They make assumptions on the perceptions they have on any given situation at the time. But where alcohol and drug abuse have lived, it can be very painful for family members to talk about the truth of that.

We are bombarded from the outside with advertisements of how good alcohol is. But go out into city centres any day of the week and see the other side. If we were flies on the walls of many homes, we would see different stories unfolding. The comfort blanket of denial is so much easier to wrap oneself in than to look at the truth.

As I write this now, all is ok within my own family dynamics, and we all get on relatively well – as families can do. I love all of them dearly but cannot comment on how they feel about me. To be honest, it is none of my business what they think about me. It is actually none of my business what they do in their lives. It has taken a lot of 'work' to get to this point, and my human self can feel upset when there are conflicting ideas about subjects within my family. But I can now see their journey too, and I feel compassion for them.

How did I manage this? By seeing their inner child and the innocence in that archetype within them, compassion has risen in me for myself and, hence, also for them. For all of humanity.

I try to see the child and see that they, too, have conditioned programmes running through them from their stories. We all have a story to tell. One of mine is that there is always someone worse off than me. That mindset actually prevented me many times from writing my story. I was normalising a living environment that truly is unacceptable for children to be brought up in by feeling that others have it much worse. For fuck's sake, it was hell! No child should have to have any type of abuse bestowed upon them. NONE!

Everyone has an opinion on others' stories and remembers individuals as they were. 'Gosh! You don't change, do you?' is a common phrase. But until we delve into our own stories and our own truths, we have no right to make judgments on others; we do, though. Me included. The difference now is that I am aware of this human condition and can change my attitude accordingly. It's not easy at times, but it is truly freeing and loving when it happens.

There is a saying that we enter into 'the dark night of the Soul' to experience our deep hurts, and our shadow selves come to the surface to be shown the light of what is really our true essence. My own personal journey threw up some nasty parts of me I had not known were there, but always the treasure of my Soul would eventually shine through once these parts were owned and, more especially, loved.

At first, I wanted to dismiss them or put them into a box, as some therapies suggest. But that wasn't a good thing for me, because the box can open, and these feelings and behaviours will erupt like a volcano and cause all sorts of bother. Actually accepting and owning these flaws meant they lost their power and did not return as often as before.

Final Thoughts

*'I don't like to face problems head on. I think the best
way to solve problems is to avoid them. In fact, this is
a distinct philosophy of mine. No problem is so big or
complicated that it can't be run away from!'*
Linus said to Charlie Brown

Denial is in constant use within society as a whole. It keeps us warm and secure by not having to look at our lives so that we can keep pointing those fingers and judging others. It keeps us from getting hurt emotionally.

It's engrained in our psyche, with deep foundations – set up from childhood – which are unmoving until we are sometimes catapulted, other times slowly, into waking up. Then it can become even more painful to move through. It takes a very courageous person to see that their denial is really a stepping-stone to a bridge of compassion for self and others. Like the snake shedding its skin, it takes time to let go. But it leads us to our Soul.

It took me two years to totally accept my own denial, and then some! More and more layers then needed to come off. That deep denial of one's own life, then the life of their family origins and behaviours. This, I believe, is when family members often part from each other.

Some members choose to remain in the denial, even when they know the truth of a situation, as it is so much easier to stay in the familiar. I totally understand that.

But the truth is so much easier once it's known, and it has definitely been healthier for me. My body has reacted to this and I have never felt better. I have aches and pains sometimes and my body will release what it doesn't need, but I continue to listen deeply to what it tells me and act accordingly.

To be in the natural flow of the Universe is our number one purpose. To know the truth of who we are and to remember that we are spiritual beings having an experience in a human body. The body is simply the vehicle to grow and expand our souls.

MOTHERS and FATHERS

Thoughts of 'not being good enough' are engrained into our societies. Like the mother who cannot bring herself to say the word 'alcoholic' on finally recognising her child is addicted to alcohol. Or the father who cannot say the words 'drug addict' or 'heroin addict', because it is too painful to admit this. These responses are often because the situation has triggered the mother or father's own insecurities from childhood and adolescent years, and they now take the addiction as a personal 'attack' on their parenting, as we have deep issues of not being good enough.

But I cannot stress enough that there is no-one to blame. And in this case, the saying that 'some things are better left unsaid' is ridiculous and one reason why we have so many problems in society today. And you could include other sayings we've all heard, like 'swept under the carpet' and 'the big white elephant in the middle of the room that everyone avoids'.

Alcohol is a legal drug which is accepted in society and makes millions of pounds in taxes for governments and the companies who make and sell it, but thousands and thousands have died of alcoholism or alcohol-related illness. Personally, I only ever took alcohol for effect and to fit in with what others were doing, as my belief system told me it was quite normal and everyone I mixed with could drink to extremes. I did not think anything was wrong with that until it became a problem for me.

When I embarked on the 12 Step Programme, it led me back to the Spirit within, the Spirit body which needed resurrected. I do believe now that this was the opening of the door; the opening to myself through having to fall into the darkest parts of my inner worlds. My martyrdom, my narcissistic, arrogant, and self-centred ways had to come to the surface through living with the dis-ease of alcoholism, and then they had to be weeded out and accepted.

Each time another layer showed itself to me, better things would emerge, and I would recognise that it was not my doing but something else guiding me. I called this my Higher Power (HP) as I still could not say the word God. Religious trauma was also embedded within as a belief, and this has also been a journey for me. It is said there is no destination, only the journey. But for me, there are many destinations, and I have to stay there while my body adjusts within to the insights that occur.

TYPES

It is said that there are four types of alcoholics, and these are set out in the book which is known in AA as The Big Book of Alcoholics Anonymous. The organisation was co-founded by Bill Wilson in 1935, and initially was only for alcoholics of a certain type. But he then came to realise that for AA to be accessible for the collective, the membership had to change.

The only requirement for membership was the desire to stop drinking, but Bill W realised that one could see the 'bottom' before actually hitting it, and that's where the different types of alcoholic – from functioning to street drunks – came in.

In the beginning of this fellowship, one was interviewed to attend the meetings, so not everyone was eligible to attend. Now we believe that AA is filled with people who maybe are not eligible to reach a rock bottom, and so the message of Bill W and others has become distorted and lost. The principles of the programme are the same as they always have been, but the message from them has been lost – it's 'hip' to be part of a 12 Step movement, thanks to a number of celebrities writing about it in their autobiographies.

In some cases, this can help the ordinary public. One who comes to mind, who I was previously not a fan of (he must have been showing me my own shit!), is the actor and comedian Russell Brand. I know many others who did not like this man, but by owning up to his shit through the movement of the 12 Steps, he has brought attention to the public in the UK around his own recovery. His book Recovery is a fantastic read, and I love how he talked about what the steps are for him and his journey through them. He has even reinvented them.

On the whole, the programme of AA works fine, but there has been some controversy over its affiliations with other 12 Step movements, like CA and NA (Cocaine and Narcotics Anonymous). Many 12 Step programmes actually use the Big Book in their meetings, but Al Anon does not. It is a separate entity but co-operates with AA and participates at their conventions. Along with the 12 Steps (which is for the individual), there are 12 Traditions (for the groups to run smoothly), and the 12 Concepts (for the worldwide groups, or collective). And these 36 principles can be worked into an individual's life to help one realise love of self, love of others, and love of the world at large.

If these principles were to be incorporated into governments and institutions, I don't doubt they would run more smoothly. However, wherever there are large organisations, there are people – humans who unfortunately will not or cannot dig deep into their psyche enough to clean up their core wounds to function and own up to their defects of character and flaws. Their intellect takes over, instead of their intelligence.

Once the journey from the head to the heart has taken place, the world becomes a more peaceful place. But in my experience, this starts with the individual.

In Carl Jung's part in the beginnings of the AA movement, he said that 'no human power' could stop someone from drinking and that a Divine intervention was needed. Look at Robert as an example. He has admitted that he could not stop drinking, yet in a 24-hour period the compulsion had been removed from him to drink alcohol. How was that? It had to be a power bigger than him that intervened for this to happen.

Sometimes there are those who return to have another go, or to research for themselves the demons of the spirit. I love how some alcoholic drinks are called spirits! Spirits can make people funny, enjoy themselves, have a laugh, and release their inhibitions, but they can also rob families of their loved ones, instil disease into the body, and kill. We are bombarded with ads on the media that alcohol will show us a good time, and we queue to buy it in the name of having fun. Yet the dark side of it quietly seeps into the psyche and destroys people and families in its wake. I find it strange that people who bang on about food and taking care of our bodies still pour copious amounts of alcohol down their necks and do not see the effects.

Nicotine has long been known for its harmful properties, so why is it treated differently from alcohol? It took around 50 years for the effects of tobacco to be told, and now cigarettes are not on show in supermarkets and have images on packets to encourage people to quit.

When there is a friend or a family member who indulges overly with alcohol or any other drug, and their resulting behaviour causes upset to others, the one who has the problem will deny they have an issue and refuse to discuss it with others. Maybe they appear to be happy-go-lucky types and everyone loves their actions, especially at family get-togethers where they are the life and soul of the party. But this behaviour can take place every weekend, and the close family member sees another side of the person, particularly if they decide to stay at home and not indulge with the drinker.

In my case, because I was a drinker anyway, I chose the attitude 'if you can't beat them join them', especially when I was physically unable to hold down a job due to undergoing the hospital appointments and surgeries after my accident.

The person abusing the substance dismisses comments from friends and family as nonsense and lies, and they fabricate stories to provide a perfectly reasonable excuse for their behaviour. You often find that the drug abuser/ drinker becomes a pathological liar who really does believe their own lies. This denial lies deep within them, and their addiction turns into a monster when confronted about their lies. This person could be very successful and self-sufficient and show a different side to the outside world than the one he/she portrays at home. But they show a change in character if questioned on what they are doing. This often means that other family members and friends become wary of them, thereby joining in the denial.

There are no one size fits all, of course. These people can also seem to be responsible by doing 'normal' things, like keeping down a good job, owning their homes, and doing lots of great family activities. Yet their family is really in denial and despair while carrying on smiling and telling others how wonderfully well their loved one is doing. This is shame in denial.

If this continues, there eventually comes a crisis at some point, which will be covered up by the others. The addict will expect others to do things for them and cry that no-one helps them when the progression of their addictions increases.

Alcoholics do not believe they have the same issue as the person they see who is perhaps smoking heroin. Both these people see the other as worse than them, and believe this gives them the right to judge. I'm not judging here, just offering what have been my observations over the 18 years of my own recovery and denial.

It took me around eight years to uproot my own denial. I was a child stuck in a woman's body, screaming for emotional help. My spirit had gone to ground from birth to the age of 14, and only started to crawl back to life when I entered the doors of the 12 Step Programme. And it took many examinations for me to come to this realisation.

Then I had to move deeper within my psyche to see that whatever I was doing affected the whole of humanity. The collective consciousness. As individuals, we affect all around us, and whatever we do will affect others. Always, and in all ways.

I was an enabler who wanted to help others out of their pain. Especially my family. Others play the part of enabler, where family are concerned, by denying their loved one has an issue. They can take the drug-taking or drinking personally: 'I've failed as a mother because my child is an addict.' So, they make it about them instead of the suffering 'child'.

As a provoker, the person who is repeatedly hurt by episodes of drinking or even withdrawal from others' substances is usually a wife, husband, or parent/guardian. This person feeds back resentment, frustration, and bitterness into the family. They will aim to show that all is well and try to force changes for the addict. But when they don't give up, they become martyrs and managers to the addict. The addict will expect them to do and be whatever they ask.

As we are all 'trained' to play out particular roles in society throughout our lives, we tend to rescue others to satisfy our own underlying motives of looking for love. It can look like the addict is a responsible adult because this one person will aim to 'fix' the crisis after it occurs. They will bail out the addict with money, with stories to others about how all is well, even though others can see through the denial. I did not know I was in any denial until I was out of it.

The addict will deny any dependency or that they are an addict (to whatever choice of drug that is). I've witnessed others admitting that they are an addict but insisting they have their addiction under control, it's not a problem for them, and deny they have trouble in their life because of it. The addict will shout from the rooftops how wonderful they are at their work, how they are the best skilled person there, and claim that other members of the family are crazy or liars. They point a finger at everyone else or something else as the reason why they need to partake in their choice of drug. Some even go so far as to take goods from their home to pawn or sell just to keep their habit going, yet still deny it.

Families do not speak to one another, sometimes until death, because the person who has left the denial chooses not to be involved around the chaos or crisis any more.

Some family members will refuse point blank to discuss anything once in recovery. It is so painful for them to be reminded how their behaviour has hurt others that they can only go into deep silence about it all. The addict may not recall what they did, but their own guilt and shame is unbearable. As a result, the addict will deny they will 'use' a substance again; the enabler will deny they will rescue again; the victim will say they will not be involved with them again; and the provoker will threaten to leave if it happens again. And so the merry-go-round continues.

The only way for an addict to remove their mental anguish is to 'use' again and again, and the only way for the family or friends to relieve their mental anguish is to verbalise and vent at the addict. Unfortunately, over years this just increases the mental anguish on both sides, and the only way to stop this train of denial is for one person to leave at the next station (metaphorically speaking), or to hop off this merry-go-round when it slows down enough to see the window of opportunity to do this. Sometimes there needs to be a train wreck – as in my case – to be able to stagger from, and it can take some time to recover. I found myself disempowered in the four aspects of physical, mental, emotional, and spiritual. Each of these environments had to be dealt with (still do) as they showed themselves.

In the beginning, I asked a friend how I could help myself and was told to do the opposite of what I would usually do. I put this into practice immediately, and had many slips, scrapes, and falls through trial and error. I had no idea that I was emotionally crippled from conditioning patterns from ancestral happenings and the society I lived in.

I had to find new roles to play and integrate them into my life, and I did this by hanging out with people who had already done it. I threw myself into the 12 Step Programme to the best of my ability, noting the changes as they occurred. I loved the 'take what you like and leave the rest' advice told to me at the end of meetings. Others would advise, 'leave the rest till later', because as I evolved through the fellowship I saw that something I did not like at the beginning was working in me now and making my life feel better. I was feeling better.

My thinking was not always good, and then I noticed I would feel like shit. I also realised that what I put into my body had an effect on how I felt. But it was hard for me to see how I contributed to sustaining the dis-ease of alcoholism within my family unit. I never knew there was such a thing as the Family Disease of Alcoholism, and that you do not need to drink to suffer from it. I never knew that so many involved with an alcoholic could be affected when that person picked up a drink, and the ripple effect through the family. I never knew it could set up a merry-go-round of blame and denial.

Alcohol can lighten us up to dance the night away or to sit with friends and reminisce of old times and good times; we laugh and joke and enjoy our time together, then go home at the end of an evening. We salute others and make toasts at events to celebrate lives, and we drink to wash our remorse away when a loved one leaves the planet. We use alcohol and drugs to cope with emotions we cannot allow to move through our bodies. We hold the pain in. We deny we are hurting.

Al Anon gave me the 12 Steps and suggestions to have my own personal programme of recovery. For this, I am eternally grateful.

My Wish For You

'Life isn't about finding yourself.
Life is about creating yourself.'
George Bernard Shaw

Each day may throw up circumstances we are not prepared for, but becoming more aware of your own inner world will allow you to seek a solution within your own heart. You are never alone; know that to be a truth. There are many people in this world willing to assist you to find your way. There are many who are not. To navigate the inner workings of your mind and heart and to connect the two, takes some doing. To heal the past's wounding is one of the greatest journeys to take. It may be easy for me to say this from where I am today, but I would not change any of it, thanks to the valuable life lessons I have been given. Lessons that became gifts.

I am not perfect, and not everyone will like or appreciate me, but that's ok. It's none of my business what others' opinions are about me. I must learn to love myself, stop complaining about others and what they do or do not do, because all I can rely on is the unexpected to occur!

I have learned that not everyone will say what they mean and be there for me, and it's not always about me. I have learned to stand alone, to take care of myself, and to champion myself into feeling safe and secure within. I aim to accept people as they are and to overlook their shortcomings (most of the time!) through forgiveness. I have learned to be open to new points of view and ideas by redefining and renewing my thoughts. I have learned the difference between wanting and needing, and have let go of past dogma and doctrines that I should never have brought along because I knew them to be BS!

I learned to stop consuming for a quick fix, and now aim to be honest in all my endeavours. It is not my job to save others, and I cannot fix them. I have learned about love and see relationships as they are and not how I want them to be.

I have seen the joy in letting go and letting God. I have learned discernment, and know what is mine and what is another's, the importance of setting boundaries, and when to say NO. I have learned to listen to my body and know my needs and another's needs. I am still learning this one.

I have learned to care for my body and treat it with respect (most of the time), and I drink copious amounts of water, exercise, and know to really listen to my body's signals. I understand that tiredness fuels doubt and uncertainty. I love to laugh and play with others, and have learned that what I put into my life I get back double. Life really is a self-fulfilling prophecy! I learned I need direction to feel successful. I need to be disciplined and ask for help when I need it, and not be a martyr. It is ok to ask for help.

I learned there is no-one punishing me but myself. Everything is not another's fault. It is life happening as life does. I now admit when I am wrong, and make amends accordingly. I want to build bridges not walls. I know what will suffocate my life and feel what I need to, until I can come through. I take 100% responsibility for myself today and, with courage, I take a deep breath and keep walking.

Please take what you like from my story and leave the rest.

I love you and wish you change and peace in your heart. I choose to follow the calling of my Soul in whatever way that manifests. I urge you to follow your Soul, too. It's an amazing journey... if you allow it.

Letter to the reader

Dear Reader

Firstly, thank you thank you thank you for reading my book. This means so much to me. If it has touched you or you know someone else you feel may benefit, please pass it on.

As I write today our world is a very different place. We are in the midst of change and transformation globally. We are all in this together as a collective humanity.

There are many different opinions as there are voices in our world, yet we realise how much we need each other now more than ever. Domestic violence and alcoholism/ addictions have increased immensely in this period so this book is about to hit the world where it could save someone like you or someone you love if they choose to seek help.

I continue to keep up with my Holistic Health through deep diving with various teachers and mentors as I now we all need support through life. I have developed my own six-week mentorship course where many others have taken the plunge to change their lives when they reached a place in their lives that they felt stuck.

If this sounds like something you would love check it out at www.lornamunro.weebly.com and I also have www. holistichealthinverness.co.uk where you can check out how I play in the world. I can still offer online sessions even with the world as it is presently. You can get in touch through either of these sites.

I am passionate about health in the four aspects as they are all interconnected. Mental, physical, emotional and spiritual. Many have had their spirits smacked from them at a young age so to re-ignite that fire within is imperative for Holistic Health. I have trained in many modalities and continue with my own personal journey so I can help others with theirs as a mentor/Soul-friend and fellow traveller in life.

My mission is to meet with others who are passionate about their health too so we can have collaboration and conscious communities who want to change the world by being the change themselves. I have witnessed the ripple effect on others when we do this. I bid you wellness and much love as you step into your wholeness.

Lorna.